Oxford English for Careers

TECHNOLOGY 1

David Bonamy
with additional material by Norman Glendinning

Teacher's Resource Book

OXFORD
UNIVERSITY PRESS

OXFORD
UNIVERSITY PRESS

Great Clarendon Street, Oxford OX2 6DP

Oxford University Press is a department of the University of Oxford.
It furthers the University's objective of excellence in research, scholarship,
and education by publishing worldwide in

Oxford   New York

Auckland Cape Town Dar es Salaam Hong Kong Karachi
Kuala Lumpur Madrid Melbourne Mexico City Nairobi
New Delhi Shanghai Taipei Toronto

With offices in

Argentina Austria Brazil Chile Czech Republic France Greece
Guatemala Hungary Italy Japan Poland Portugal Singapore
South Korea Switzerland Thailand Turkey Ukraine Vietnam

OXFORD and OXFORD ENGLISH are registered trade marks of
Oxford University Press in the UK and in certain other countries

© Oxford University Press 2007

The moral rights of the author have been asserted

Database right Oxford University Press (maker)

First published 2007

2018 2017 2016 2015 2014
10 9 8 7 6 5

All rights reserved. No part of this publication may be reproduced,
stored in a retrieval system, or transmitted, in any form or by any means,
without the prior permission in writing of Oxford University Press (with
the sole exception of photocopying carried out under the conditions stated
in the paragraph headed 'Photocopying'), or as expressly permitted by law, or
under terms agreed with the appropriate reprographics rights organization.
Enquiries concerning reproduction outside the scope of the above should
be sent to the ELT Rights Department, Oxford University Press, at the
address above

You must not circulate this book in any other binding or cover
and you must impose this same condition on any acquirer

Photocopying

The Publisher grants permission for the photocopying of those pages marked
'photocopiable' according to the following conditions. Individual purchasers
may make copies for their own use or for use by classes that they teach.
School purchasers may make copies for use by staff and students, but this
permission does not extend to additional schools or branches

Under no circumstances may any part of this book be photocopied for resale

Any websites referred to in this publication are in the public domain and
their addresses are provided by Oxford University Press for information only.
Oxford University Press disclaims any responsibility for the content

ISBN: 978 0 19 456951 4

Printed in China

ACKNOWLEDGEMENTS

The authors and publisher are grateful to the following for their permission to reproduce photographs and illustrative material: Alamy Images p.92 (Photos.com Select/ JupiterMedia); Corbis pp.74 (woman with headphones), 77 (ImageSource), 84 (Toshiyuki Aizawa/Reuters); Getty Images pp.70 (family car/Dustin Hardin/ Stone), 70 (sports car/Peter Cade/Iconica), p.96 (Nick Dolhing/Taxi); Muji p.74 (CD player); OUP p.83 (cheese, sweets/Hemera); Punchstock p.94 (satellite/ DigitalVision); Punchstock/Veer (cover image); Rex Features pp.83 (sweet factory), 88 (radiologist); Science Photo Library p.83 (cheese making/ Maximilian Stock Ltd)

Illustrations by: Peter Bull Arts Studio

Contents

Introduction p.4

Background, teaching notes, tips, and additional activities

1 Technology and society p.6
2 Studying technology p.10
3 Design p.14
4 Technology in sport p.18
5 Appropriate technology p.22
6 Crime-fighting and security p.26
7 Manufacturing p.30
8 Transport p.34
9 High living: skyscrapers p.38
10 Medical technology p.42
11 Personal entertainment p.46
12 Information technology p.50
13 Telecommunications p.55
14 Careers in technology p.59
15 The future of technology p.62

Grammar tests and communication activities

Instructions for communication activities p.66

1 Technology and society p.70
2 Studying technology p.72
3 Design p.74
4 Technology in sport p.76
5 Appropriate technology p.78
6 Crime-fighting and security p.80
7 Manufacturing p.82
8 Transport p.84
9 High living: skyscrapers p.86
10 Medical technology p.88
11 Personal entertainment p.90
12 Information technology p.92
13 Telecommunications p.94
14 Careers in technology p.96
15 The future of technology p.98

Grammar tests key p.100

Introduction

Technology is aimed at preparing students who intend to get a job in technology. It presents them with English from a wide variety of technological fields and situations, develops their communication skills, and provides them with background in major technological concepts.

Switch on

This is designed as a warm-up activity to the unit. It usually consists of a number of pictures, and often introduces key vocabulary or concepts. It should be used to get students to focus on the topic.

It's my job

These occur regularly, either as a reading or listening exercise. They are all based on authentic interviews and sources and are designed to be of interest to the students as they stand with only minimal tasks. Students will read about a variety of young people in different technology environments and gain insight into the skills required.

General focus questions for *It's my job* are: *What do you think his / her job involves? What skills and experience does he / she need? Would you like to do it?*

As an ongoing project, encourage the class to build up a portfolio of other *It's my job* features. For example, if students know someone who works in technology, they can write their own *It's my job* article or interview, with photos.

Customer care

Increasingly in technology, it is not enough to have technical skills, qualifications, and knowledge of the field. The ability to write clearly and present ideas in speech is also important. A high proportion of communication will be with fellow specialists, but there will be times when students will have to communicate about technical matters with non-specialists such as clients, visitors, and customers. This can be much more demanding. The *Customer care* feature gives students practice in this important 'soft skill'.

Problem-solving

This encourages students to work together to solve a problem – a key skill in technology. It is designed to stimulate discussion, and often involves ranking exercises or evaluating the practicality of a variety of solutions to a particular problem.

Top margin

This top part of the page contains facts, statistics, and quotes. These are optional extras and can be used to add variety and interest to your lessons, or provide additional material for strong students who are 'fast finishers'. Ways of exploitation include asking whether your students are surprised by the facts and statistics, or whether they agree, disagree, or can identify with the quotes.

It also contains *Gadget box*: interesting, often quirky, technological innovations related to the unit topic. Each *Gadget box* has an associated question, and allows you to take time out from the flow of the lesson in order to promote a more open-ended discussion.

There are also definitions for difficult words or phrases which are important to understand a text which appears on the same page. (Words or phrases in the text are highlighted in **bold**.)

Vocabulary

Students meet a large amount of vocabulary during the course. It is important to encourage good learning skills from the start, for example:
- organizing vocabulary into word sets and word groups rather than simple alphabetical lists
- understanding the context of vocabulary and whether it is a key word needed for production or for comprehension
- checking and learning the pronunciation of a word or phrase.

Language spot

This focuses on the grammar that is generated by the topic of the unit and concentrates on its practical application.

If your students need revision after completing the *Language spot*, direct them to the *Grammar reference*, which provides a handy check.

There is also one photocopiable *Grammar test* for each unit in this Teacher's Resource Book.

Listening, Reading, Speaking / Pairwork, Writing

These activities give realistic and communicative practice of language skills needed in technology.

- In the listening activities students are exposed to situations related to technology, including dialogues, technical explanations, and interviews. They also hear a variety of English accents, both native speaker and non-native speaker.
- In the reading sections students meet a variety of technology-based texts (see Reading bank).
- In the speaking and pairwork sections, try to ensure use of English during activities, particularly those involving some discussion. Encourage this by teaching or revising any functional language students may need. There is also one photocopiable *Communication activity* for each unit in this Teacher's Resource Book.
- Writing practice in the units is designed as consolidation and extension of the topic with structured, meaningful writing tasks.

Pronunciation

This practises aspects of pronunciation which are of maximum importance for intelligibility.

You can repeat the recordings in the *Pronunciation* as often as you like until you and your students feel confident they have mastered a particular sound or feature.

Project / Webquest

These encourage students to take an active role in the learning process, both in terms of their English language work and the subject of technology itself.

Projects can be set as homework assignments, but it is worth spending time in class preparing students for the task. In *Webquests* students are usually required to use search engines such as www.google.com to find information, as well as websites dedicated to technological issues. Help can also be given by brainstorming some standard places where they can gather information.

Checklist

This allows students to check their own progress. You may want to get students to grade or assess how well they can perform each of the 'Can do' statements, e.g. 'easily', 'with difficulty', or 'not at all'. They can also test each other in pairs, by giving examples from the unit of each of the 'Can do' statements.

Key words

These are the main items of technology vocabulary introduced in the unit. A definition of each of these words appears in the *Glossary*. You should certainly check students' pronunciation, including the stress, of words likely to be used orally.

This section also provides students with the opportunity to look back through the unit and note anything about how English is used in technology that is new to them. In addition to encouraging students to build their own personal vocabulary, this activity encourages them to reflect.

Reading bank

This is in the middle of the book and gives specific skills practice in reading. The ability to read and understand texts in English has never been more important in technology than it is today with the amount of written information available on the Internet, the majority of which is in English. The reading texts are accompanied by pre-reading tasks and comprehension questions. The texts can be used throughout the course, either in class, or as self-study or homework. There is also an *Answer key* in the Student's Book to encourage students to check their work.

Pairwork activities

This section contains one or more parts of the information gap activities from the main units (see *Speaking / Pairwork*).

Grammar reference

This can be used together with the *Language spot*, as a handy check or revision. It shows the form of a particular grammar point, briefly explains its use, and provides example sentences as well as indicating likely student errors.

Listening scripts

This is a complete transcript of all the recordings. Direct students to it for checking answers after they have completed a *Listening* task, or allow weaker students to read it as they listen to a particular recording, perhaps for a final time.

Glossary

This is an alphabetical list of all the *Key words*. Each word is followed by the pronunciation in phonetic script, the part of speech, and a definition in English.

The section begins with a phonetic chart, with an example word from technology to illustrate each of the sounds.

1 Technology and society

Background

The purpose of technology is to produce applications which improve our material environment. The people who design, test, and make these applications are called technicians, technologists, and engineers. They work in areas such as civil, mechanical, electrical, electronic, and marine engineering, and in newer fields such as information technology (IT). They use scientific knowledge and technological experience in their work. They often adapt older existing technology (e.g. radio waves) to create new applications (e.g. mobile phones).

Technology is all around us and affects every aspect of our lives. Here are some examples:

- **transport** – road, sea, and air travel; space exploration
- **telecommunications** – mobile phones, fibre optics, internet, satellites
- **trade** – credit and debit cards, bank ATM machines, business-to-business (B2B) internet trade
- **work efficiency** – washing machines, microwave ovens, computer software
- **power** – heating, lighting, air conditioning
- **personal entertainment** – DVDs, iPods, digital TVs, digital cameras
- **health** – lasers in eye surgery, medicines
- **safety and security** – ABS brakes, air bags, sensors, smoke detectors
- **food** – food processing, agriculture
- **information management** – computer databases, search engines, business software
- **infrastructure** – roads, buildings, sewerage, waste disposal, water supply
- **manufacturing** – robotics in mass production (manufacturing an item in very large numbers)

Because technology is so important in society, technicians, technologists, and engineers always have to think about values, that is, whether something is good or bad. Unfortunately, some technology has both positive and negative effects on society. Using minerals such as oil, coal, iron, and uranium improves our standard of living, but can also pollute the air, water, and ground. The same rockets that allow space exploration can carry nuclear weapons. Road vehicles and planes allow fast travel but also cause accidental deaths and create global warming. The challenge for technology is how to increase the positive effects on society but reduce or eliminate the negative effects.

✱ Tip

effect v affect
These sentences mean the same:
1 What is the effect of technology on society?
2 How does technology affect society?
Here, *effect* is a noun and *affect* is the related verb.

Switch on

1 Encourage a short discussion about each picture, and how the technology affects our lives.

2 Refer students again to Picture A, the rocket. Ask: *Does this have a mainly positive or negative effect on our lives?* Encourage a short discussion, and get students to consider both sides, see example – *Positive effect: space exploration, Negative effect: nuclear missiles*. Then get students to do the matching exercise.

Picture	Positive	Negative
B	11	6
C	5	10
D	4	2
E	1	7
F	12	9

Encourage stronger students to produce fuller answers. For example:

Item	Positive effects	Negative effects
A rocket	space exploration, satellites launched for weather forecasting, global positioning, etc. nuclear deterrent	nuclear weapons, arms race, pollution in space, huge expenditure for little result

* Tip
Internet v intranet
Internet – a world-wide computer network.
intranet – a computer network in a single organization.

* Tip
Plastic money
Credit cards and *debit cards* are often called *'plastic'* in everyday English.

* Tip
Spelling rules

Rule	Simple	Comparative
Short adjectives		
Add *-er*	quiet	quieter
Short adjectives ending in *e*		
Add *-r*	wide	wider
Short adjectives ending in vowel + consonant		
Double final letter and add *-er*	thin	thinner
Short adjectives ending in *y*		
Change final *-y* to *-i* and add *-er*	heavy	heavier
good, bad, far		
Change the word (irregular)	good	better
Long adjectives		
Use *more*	expensive	more expensive

* Tip
A *turbofan* is a jet engine
A *Newton* is a unit of force

* Tip
Numbers and units
397,246.05kg is said as:
three hundred and ninety-seven thousand two hundred and forty-six point oh five kilograms
Point out:
- the comma is not spoken
- the decimal point is said as *point*
- the numbers after the point are given as separate digits
- 0 after the point can be said as *oh* or as *zero*
- although *kg* is written as singular, it is spoken as plural

Listening
Technology and work

1 🎧 Before listening, discuss the meaning of the following terms with students: *Internet* and *intranet* (see *Tip*). Show a credit or debit card to elicit *credit card* and *debit card* (see *Tip*).

Play the whole recording through once and ask students to match the people to the jobs.

1 b   2 d   3 a   4 c

2 🎧 Tell students to listen again and decide if the speaker thinks the technology is positive, or negative, or both.

Speaker	Positive	Negative
1 Vera	✓	
2 Christine	✓	
3 Gupta	✓	✓
4 Anton		✓

3 🎧 Play the recording of just the shop owner again, and put students in pairs to write down what he says. Then let them check their answers with the *Listening script* in the Student's Book on p.124.

Language spot
Comparisons with adjectives and adverbs

Check students understand the difference between adjectives and adverbs. Ask them to make simple sentences using *fast, early, high,* and *late* as both adverbs and adjectives. For example: *This is a fast train* (adjective), and *The train goes very fast* (adverb).

1 Before doing the exercise, ask students to say which adjectives will change their spelling according to the rules in the *Tip* table (*large, big, heavy*).

2 faster	6 smaller	10 more sophisticated
3 larger	7 cheaper	11 more efficiently
4 bigger	8 lower	
5 less heavy	9 better	

2 Check students understand the information in the table. Then get students to make some sentences orally comparing the two planes using comparative adjectives. Finally, set the exercise.

| 1 longer | 3 heavier | 5 farther / further | 7 more powerful |
| 2 shorter | 4 faster | 6 higher | 8 more recently |

8 Unit 1

➕ Additional activity
(weaker students)
Put weaker students into two groups. Students take it in turns to read out the raw data. (This is a useful check that they can 'translate' the written numbers and unit abbreviations into words.) If a student reads it correctly, he / she gets one point. If the opposite group think the student has made a mistake, and correct it, they get two points.

➕ Additional activity
(stronger students)
Encourage students to produce additional sentences using a wider range of structures, for example:
- *The Boeing has a smaller capacity than the Airbus.*
- *The Airbus has the same number of engines as the Boeing.*
- *The Airbus is slightly slower than the Boeing.*

✱ Tip
text message – written words sent via mobile phone (also called SMS)
microwave – a high-frequency electromagnetic wave, used in microwave ovens
hack – gain illegal access to a computer
Apple – the name of a computer company

✱ Tip
Sensors
ionization: giving an atom an electric charge
optical: using light waves
detect (v) = *sense* (v)
detector (n) = *sensor* (n)

➕ Additional activity
(stronger students)
Put students into groups to produce a large-scale simple diagram of either 1) the optical detector smoke alarm, or 2) the ionization detector smoke alarm. This can be prepared as homework. They can then present their diagram to the class and give a short oral explanation of how it works.

3 If necessary do this orally first, then get students to write their sentences.

Reading
Branches of technology

First check that students understand the following words in the news stories (see *Tip*).

🔑 1 a   2 g   3 b   4 c   5 f   6 d   7 h   8 e

Vocabulary
Recording new words

These tasks introduce students to two useful ways of learning and remembering key technical vocabulary: word sets and word cards. Encourage students to keep a record of new technical vocabulary in special notebooks and on word cards.

1 Ask students to produce the word sets in pairs.

2 Ask students to produce word cards individually, with a good dictionary. If possible, use this as an opportunity to encourage use of an English–English dictionary.

Gadget box

🔑 In corridors near bedrooms

When students have completed *Project: class survey* ask them if they were surprised that the smoke detector was top of the UK survey list. Ask them why they think it was top (possible answer: *It saves a lot of lives and is found in many homes.*)

Pronunciation
Word stress

🎧 Get students to listen to the words and mark the stressed syllables. Tell them to notice cases where the stress changes according to the part of speech. For example, in *ma<u>chine</u>* and *ma<u>chin</u>ery* there is no change, but in *<u>tech</u>nical* and *tech<u>ni</u>cian* the stressed syllable changes.

🔑 1 ma<u>chine</u>   5 me<u>chan</u>ical   9 e<u>lec</u>tron
    2 ma<u>chin</u>ery   6 <u>tech</u>nical   10 elec<u>tron</u>ics
    3 me<u>chan</u>ics   7 tech<u>ni</u>cian   11 e<u>lec</u>trical
    4 me<u>chan</u>ic   8 tech<u>nol</u>ogy   12 elec<u>tri</u>cian

Vocabulary
Word groups

This exercise introduces students to another way of learning and remembering key technical vocabulary.

Technology and society

Subjects	People and jobs	Things	Adjectives
mechanics	mechanic	mechanism	mechanical
electronics	–	electron	electronic
technology	technician	–	technical
–	electrician	electricity	electrical

Pairwork

Before dividing students into pairs for this task, briefly discuss the headings in the left-hand column of the table and check their understanding. *Payload* means paid cargo. *Geostationary* satellites orbit the Earth at the speed of the Earth's rotation (and so appear stationary from Earth). There is more information about satellites and orbit in Unit 13, p.96.

Project: class survey

1 Put students into small groups. Ask students to order the items individually first, and then discuss with their group and agree a final order (see *Webquest* key). Ask groups if they were surprised by the UK survey findings. Discuss the innovations briefly, and check that students understand all the terms (see *Tip*).

2 Tell students they can choose some innovations from the list in **1** or choose different ones. Get each group to decide on four or five innovations, then have a class discussion to decide the top ten.

* Tip
Some innovations
ABS (Antilock Braking System) – prevents a vehicle from skidding when you brake.
air bag – this inflates when a car crashes, and protects the driver.
DNA – the material inside cells that carries genetic information.
laser – a narrow, intense beam of light which is powerful enough to cut things.

Webquest

Set this task as homework. Ask students to do their own research, and then compare their answers with their group in the next class.

(Note: a number of answers are possible because some innovations have different stages in their development.)

Innovation	Order	Year
Smoke detector	1	1969
Mobile phone	2	1946
Microwave oven	3	1945 / 46 / 48
Digital camera	4	1987
DNA testing	5	1985
Laser eye surgery	6	1970s
Air bags	7	early 1970s
Credit cards	8	1951
Long-life, low-energy light bulbs	9	unknown
ABS brakes	10	late 1980s

Key words

Go through the list of words to check students' pronunciation and understanding. Refer them to the *Glossary* if necessary.

➕ Additional activity
(stronger students)
Ask students to think of ways of grouping some of the *Key words* with related words. For example: *affect* (v) with *effect* (n); *download* with its opposite *upload*; *exploration* (n) with *explore* (v); *innovation* (n) with *innovate* (v); *pollution* (n) with *pollute* (v); *take-off* (n) with *take off* (v) and its opposite *land* (v).

2 Studying technology

Background

What is the difference between a technician, a technologist, and an engineer? The main difference is in level of education and training. Engineers have the most advanced training and normally hold university degrees. In everyday contexts, the titles technician and technologist are sometimes used interchangeably, meaning a specialist working in technology below the level of engineer. In training contexts, technologist is normally used for someone at a higher level (usually trained for 2–3 years) than a technician (usually trained for 1–2 years).

You can progress from technician to technologist and then to engineer by following courses at colleges and universities. Colleges offer certificates and diplomas (a diploma is a higher level qualification than a certificate). Universities offer degrees.

As an example, in the UK system, most young people who want a career in technology start by studying at a college of further education or university. They would normally follow the route: HNC (Higher National Certificate) → HND (Higher National Diploma) → B.Eng /biː endʒ/ (Bachelor of Engineering degree). Some universities allow students to transfer to a degree course early, after completing only one year of a diploma course.

It is also possible for students to leave school at sixteen and work as apprentices with a company. The company can then release them from work for some time every week to allow them to study at a college. This is called a part-time, day-release or 'sandwich' course.

In this unit, there is an example of a student, Alec, who is following an HND diploma course in civil engineering in a college in Scotland. Civil engineers work in the planning and construction of airports, bridges, highways, harbours, etc. The course syllabus includes the following subjects:

- **Construction surveying.** This teaches how to measure a site, and mark out lines and points from the plans on the ground.
- **Construction management.** This teaches how to ensure that a building project is completed on time, with the correct materials, within budget, and safely.
- **Fluid mechanics.** This teaches how liquids and gases move and affect structures. This is important in constructing pipelines and dams.
- **Geotechnics.** This teaches the mechanical properties of soil and rocks. This is important in constructing tunnels, pipelines, and foundations.
- **Complex communications** (sometimes called simply communication, or communication skills). This teaches how to communicate on technical matters. Working in technology you need to be able to speak and write effectively to clients, write clear reports, and give oral presentations to colleagues.
- **CAD** (Computer-assisted design). Surveyors and architects use computer software to help them draw plans and designs.

Switch on

1 Set this first as a scanning exercise. Give students a five-minute time limit to read quickly and silently to answer the questions. Then allow them to re-read the text more slowly if necessary to check their answers.

> 1 Two years
> 2 Manager, technologist, and technician in the construction industry
> 3 Yes

2 Discuss the answers with students and check that they know what all the subjects are.

> 1 Civil engineering materials
> 2 IT
> 3 Mechanics and structure
> 4 Maths
> 5 Communications

3 Choose one or two pairs to give their answers to the questions. Refer to *What can I do next?* for the answer to 1. Discuss how engineering courses are different in their own country and ask students' opinions about this course.

Listening
The course

1 Do this exercise before students listen. The exercise will help familiarize them with the timetable.

1	09.00	3	B. Davis
2	4.5	4	Self-study

2 Play part 1 of the interview. If necessary, play the recording more than once, but play the complete section each time if possible, preferably without pausing.

1	Second semester of his first year	4	Architectural Technician
2	None	5	Graphic communication
3	Seventeen		

3 Play part 2 of the interview. Use the same procedure as in **2**. Note that the gaps do not occur on the tape in the numbered order.

1, 2	Theory of structures
3, 4	Complex communications
5	Fluid mechanics
6, 7, 8	Project work

➕ Additional activity
(stronger students)
Here are some additional questions to ask based on part 2 of the interview:
- *How is the course assessed?*
- *What project is he working on?*
- *In Complex communications, what is he writing his report about?*
- *How can a student transfer from an HND to a BEng degree?*

4 First get students to predict the answers to the questions without playing the recording. Do not check or correct their answers at this point.

Then play part 3 of the interview, using the same procedure as in **2**. (Note: the *Firth of Forth* is a long channel of the North Sea, just north of the Scottish capital, Edinburgh.)

1	Take a degree in Structural Engineering
2	BEng
3	Four years
4	Big structures

5 Get students to write their own timetables in English. Tell them to use the one in the Student's Book as a model.

Language spot
Present Simple v Present Continuous

Elicit the answer that sentences 1–4 use the Present Continuous because they describe a temporary situation. In 1, Alec is currently doing an HND, but will soon complete his course and start doing something else. In 2–4, the projects will last a limited time and then come to an end. Sentence 5 uses the Present Simple because it describes a weekly routine. Sentences 6–8 have verbs of thinking and feeling (*enjoy, like, want*).

✱ Tip
Top margin
Ask students to look at the statistic and compare it to the percentages of males and females on their course. If appropriate, discuss why men seem to be more attracted to technology than women.

1 Before students do this exercise, check that they know which tenses to use. For example, elicit that sentence 1 should be Present Simple because it expresses a daily or weekly routine. In sentence 10, point out that the Present Simple is also possible – using the Present Continuous indicates the situation is temporary until a new bridge is built.

> 1 teaches   5 studies   9 think
> 2 start   6 wants   10 is carrying
> 3 is / 's taking   7 is / 's working
> 4 is / 's studying 8 do not / don't like

2 Get students to write down the answers to these questions based on their own timetables.

3 In pairs, get students to ask and answer questions using their own timetables.

4 Get students to complete the text individually, based on their own timetables. Gap 5, after *I will get a …* , is followed by the name of the qualification. Example: *I will get a diploma*.

Pronunciation

Strong and weak forms of auxiliary verbs

1 🎧 Play the recording and discuss the examples.
Does Alec like Maths? (*Does* is not stressed: weak form)
*Yes, he **does***. (*Does* is stressed here: strong form).
Is he in his first year? (*Is* is not stressed: weak form)
*Yes, he **is***. (*Is* is stressed here: strong form).

Explain that when we answer a question that expects the answer *Yes* or *No*, we do not normally repeat the full verb of the question, but usually substitute an auxiliary verb. For example: **Q** *Do you like swimming?* **A** *Yes, I do. / No, I don't*. The words *do* and *don't* are auxiliary verbs. When auxiliary verbs are used in this way (answering a *Yes / No* question), they are stressed – this is called the *strong* form. When the auxiliary is used in the question itself, it is not normally stressed – this is called the *weak* form.

2 In pairs, get students to ask and answer each other. Make sure that students use the *weak* form in the questions, and the *strong* form in the answers.

> 1 Yes, he <u>is</u>.   3 Yes, it <u>does</u>.   5 Yes, he <u>has</u>.   7 Yes, it <u>will</u>.
> 2 No, there <u>aren't</u>. 4 No, he <u>can't</u>.   6 Yes, he <u>does</u>. 8 Yes, he <u>has</u>.

3 🎧 First, ask students to write their answers next to the questions in **2**. Then play the recording and get students to underline the strong forms. (The strong forms are underlined in the key to **2** above).

4 In pairs get students to ask and answer the questions using information about themselves and their course.

Pairwork

Get students to work in pairs, asking each other questions and completing the timetable. Walk around and check that they are using the Present Simple to ask questions such as *What subject does he / she have on Wednesdays?*

---

* Tip
Auxiliary verbs
Common auxiliary verbs include: *do, does, has, have, am, is, are, did, was, were, can, will,* and their negatives *don't,* etc.

➕ Additional activity
(weaker students)
Prepare a set of 8–10 cards, each one with a job title, for example: *Electrical Engineer, Marine Engineer, IT Technician, Mechanic, Architect,* etc. In two groups, each member of group A takes a card. Students from group B try to guess the person's job by asking *Yes / No* questions such as *Do you design houses?* Check that the answers use the strong form of auxiliaries, e.g. *Yes, I <u>do</u>.*

Problem-solving

1 Get students to do this individually first, and then to discuss their decisions with their group.

🔑 A 8   B 5   C 4   D 3   E 1   F 6   G 7   H 2

2 Get students to do this task in small groups. Encourage students to use sentences 1–8 as models for their explanations.

Webquest

1 Get students to read the course description as quickly as possible and complete the table individually.

🔑 College or University	*Hornby College of Technology*
Course	Foundation degree in Computing – Web technology
Entry qualifications	A-level but other qualifications including work experience will be considered
Length	Three years
Career prospects	Jobs in most sectors as well as web development, animation, and computer games

2 Get students to work in small groups to plan the work. Each group chooses a course and then each member then searches a different website and writes the information in a similar way to that in **1**.

3 Get students to rejoin their groups and agree on the most interesting course. They then describe the course, and the reasons for their choice, to the rest of the class.

➕ Additional activity
(stronger students)
Get students to write at least one other form of these words in tables, continuing their word study from Unit 1:
architecture, construction, manufacturing, qualification, research, structure.
For example: *architecture* (subject); *architect* (profession or person); *architectural* (adjective)

Key words

Go through the list of words to check students' pronunciation and understanding. Refer them to the *Glossary* if necessary.

3 Design

Background

Design is at the heart of technology. This is why most technology courses include design in their syllabus. Look at any manufactured product, and you will see evidence of design. It may be beautiful, but appearance is only one aspect of design. It must also function well. The design process is a series of stages, or steps. It begins when someone notices that there is a need or problem in society which must be solved. It ends when a product is manufactured which meets or fulfils that need.

These are the stages of the design process.

- **Identify the problem.** For example: When a certain cooking pot is heated, the handle becomes too hot to touch. Sometimes the designer may have to invent a new product to solve the problem. At other times he or she may modify, or change, an existing design to improve it.
- **Write the design brief** (also called the design specification). This is a simple, clear statement of what is to be designed. For example: Design a handle that remains cool when the pot is heated.
- **Do an investigation.** The designer asks questions and finds out information to help design a good product: Who will use this product? What will it do? How will it look? What materials are available? How much will they cost? Do they have the right properties (such as durability)? How will the product be made? How can it be made safe?
- **Develop alternative solutions.** Here, the designer thinks of different ideas, writing them all down without evaluating them at first. He or she will then produce sketches, or simple drawings, of the different designs.
- **Choose the best solution.** Here, the designer chooses the design which best solves the problem. He or she also considers cost, time, available materials, manufacturability (that is, whether it can be manufactured using available skills, tools, and machinery).
- **Make a model or prototype** (also called the realization stage, when a design is realized or made into a real object). A detailed drawing is made, probably using CAD software. Then a model or prototype (= first working version) is manufactured (or a computer simulation may be used).
- **Test and evaluate.** The prototype is physically tested and then evaluated to answer these questions: Does it work? Does it meet the design brief? Can it be improved in any way?
- **Manufacture.** If the final evaluation is positive, the company may decide to manufacture the product.

Switch on

Get students to discuss the products in pairs. Then get the pairs to report their ideas to the whole class. Guide discussions from appearance towards other aspects of design such as ease of use, safety, simplicity, and efficiency.

> **Possible answers**
> A headphones – almost anyone – lightness, comfort
> B cordless electric drill – DIY enthusiast, tradesperson – safety, good insulation, easy to hold and control
> C rucksack / backpack – walker, skier – lightness, waterproof, comfort
> D sports drinks bottle – sportspeople – easy to carry, easy to drink from
> E can opener – anyone – shape, comfortable to hold and use, effective
> F steering wheel – car driver – shape allows you to see dials

Listening

The design process

1 Before listening, discuss an item from *Switch on*. Ask students how they would design it and what stages they would follow. Ask them to predict some of the answers to the exercise.

✱ Tip

To explain the difference between *testing* and *evaluating*, remind them of their experience as students. First they are *tested* in an exam and then they are *evaluated* when they are given a grade.

Then set the listening and check their answers. After the task, check their understanding of the key design vocabulary. Refer to the *Background* for the meanings of *design brief/specification*, and the meaning of *realization* (= making something *real* by producing a prototype or model).

> Stage 1 e – *I start with a brief – a description of the problem I'm going to solve. In this case it's to design a backpack for cross-country skiers.*
> Stage 2 c – *Then I do some research about cross-country skiers, the things they need to carry and the weight they find comfortable. I also think about the best choice of material – waterproof, hard-wearing, easy to work with.*
> Stage 4 a – *I … choose what I think is the best solution.*
> Stage 5 d – *I transfer my sketch to a computer to make a proper drawing with all the dimensions in place. Then I ask a company to make up some prototypes.*
> Stage 7 b – *Finally I compare the product with the brief. Does it meet all the requirements? Can I make it any better?*

2 Get students to discuss the questions in pairs, and report back to the class. Discuss their answers.

> a 2   b 6   c 1   d 7   e 2   f 4   g 3   h 5   i 7

✱ Tip

Questions expecting a *Yes / No* answer usually have a *rising* intonation.
Questions expecting information (*wh-* questions) usually have a *falling* intonation.

Language spot
Question types

Get students to look again at the questions in *Listening*. Ask: *Which ones expect the answer Yes or No?* (b, f, i). Ask students what they notice about their structure (*they all have the structure **auxiliary verb + subject***). Get students to brainstorm other auxiliary verbs and write them all on the board: *is, can, does, will, are*, etc. Get them to ask *Yes / No* questions about the rucksack, the power drill, etc.

Now get students to look at the remaining questions in *Listening*. Ask them what kind of answer these questions expect (*information, not just Yes / No*). Point out that the *Wh-*question word comes at the beginning, even where it is the object of the sentence.

1 Ask students which sentences already have an auxiliary verb in them (1, 3, 5, 7, 9). Ask them what they will do in the case of sentence 2, with no auxiliary – they have to provide an appropriate auxiliary. *It works → Does it work?* Do this exercise orally and check that students use a rising intonation.

➕ Additional activity
(all levels)

After students have done exercise 1 get them to do a few in pairs as question and answer, using short forms as in Unit 2, e.g.
1 **A** Is it safe? **B** Yes, it *is*.
After students have done exercise 2 get them to do a few in pairs as question and answer, using short forms in the answer, e.g. 1 **A** Where does she work? **B** In London.

> 1 Is it safe?
> 2 Does it work well?
> 3 Can you mould some plastics easily?
> 4 Did she make a model?
> 5 Has he designed a lot of products?
> 6 Do you design sports equipment?
> 7 Are the materials available?
> 8 Did he build a prototype?
> 9 Have they drawn a lot of sketches?
> 10 Does she think nylon is the best choice?

16 Unit 3

➕ Additional activity
(all levels)
Play a version of twenty questions. In two teams, a student from Team A has to think of a gadget or piece of equipment (from this or earlier units). Students from Team B can only ask *Yes / No* questions. They are not allowed to ask what the item is directly. Check they use the correct forms and a rising intonation.

✱ Tip
Top margin
Point out the quotation from Shaw at the top of p.19. Ask students what they think is the most important quality of a designer. (Possible answers: *creativity, imagination, must be a dreamer*.) Then ask them why they think the *design brief* is so important. (Possible answer: *to make sure that the dreams are realistic and really solve the problem*.)

✱ Tip
mass-produce – to manufacture in very large quantities
durable – able to last a long time

➕ Additional activity
(weaker students)
Get students to make short sentences using the modals *should* or *must*. For example: *The chair should be lightweight, but it must be strong.*

2 After students have completed the questions, get them to say them aloud. Check they use a falling intonation.

> 🔑 1 … does she work?   6 … do you use plastic?
> 2 … did she move there?   7 … much does it weigh?
> 3 … does she design?   8 … much does it cost?
> 4 … do you work with?   9 … many functions does it have?
> 5 … do you use?   10 … can I buy it?

Customer care
Using non-specialist language

1 Discuss this with the class. Non-specialists would probably not know the meaning of such terms as *TFT XGA, 1024 by 768 pixels*, and *high-resolution*.

2 Discuss this and get students to explain why this explanation is clearer to non-specialists (*technical terms are explained and recommendations given*).

3 Get students to choose one of the topics, or a topic in their own field. Check that they are trying to clarify the specialist terms.

It's my job

1 Remind students of the design brief from *Listening*. Explain that the items in the left-hand column in this exercise form the design brief for the new garden chair. Check that students understand the terms. Then get them to do the exercise.

> 🔑 2 c   3 a   4 g   5 b   6 h   7 d   8 f

2 Before students read the text, revise the stages of the design process. Then ask them what they think Kenneth's first action would be as part of the *investigation* stage. What would he do during the *realization* stage? Next get them to read the text and compare their suggestions with Kenneth's actions. Finally, set the exercise.

> 🔑 1 durable   2 rival   3 support   4 sketches   5 mould   6 prototype

3 Get students to make a list of questions, and check that they have produced a mixture of *Yes / No* and information question types. Check also that their questions relate to some information in the text.

4 Get students to ask and answer in pairs, with one student taking Kenneth's part and answering with correct information from the text.

Gadget box

Ask students what is surprising about this information (*the product has large sales, even though it was designed 'for fun'*). Different ideas are possible for why it is successful (*it looks good, it is unusual, and it is easy to use*).

Design 17

Listening

Working with design

1 Get students to do this exercise individually, using the *Glossary* to check their answers.

2 🎧 Play each of parts A, B, and C to the class and get them to note down the answers to the questions.

> 🔑 A 1 Products for home use, especially in the kitchen
> 2 The function of the object and how people will use it
> 3 A sketch of the shape
> B 4 Mass-produced products
> 5 What people need and what it's possible to make
> 6 A sketch
> C 7 Product developer
> 8 Designers and manufacturers
> 9 The costings

3 🎧 Play part A again once to refresh students' memories, and then ask them in pairs to write down what they can remember. Then get them to check their own versions with the *Listening script* on p.125.

Problem-solving

1 Ask the whole class what the design brief is (*design a chair for use in a room intended both for lectures and for indoor sports*). Ask each group to list the advantages and disadvantages of each model, and to decide on the best design. Get groups to report back their decisions to the class.

2 Each group writes the design brief for the new chair. Then they brainstorm ideas and draw sketches for different possible designs. Finally, they decide on the best design and sketch, and present these to the whole class. The class can then vote on the best design.

Pairwork

1 Check students understand the task: Student A completes the table by asking Student B questions. Then Student B has to do the same by asking Student A.

2 Students can do this project in pairs as a homework assignment, either using a library or a computer terminal with internet access. Some basic information is given in the key below, but students may find slightly different information.

> 🔑 Alec Issigonis (1906–1988). Born in Smyrna, at that time Greek, but moved to the UK in 1923. Motor car designer, best known for the Morris Mini introduced in 1958.
> Philippe Starck (1949–). French interior designer, architect, and designer of a wide range of consumer products from toothbrushes to computers.
> Giorgetto Giugiaro (1938–). Italian designer of Nikon cameras, Seiko watches, the Volkswagen Golf, the Fiat Uno and Panda, and many other cars.

Key words

Go through the list of words to check students' pronunciation and understanding. Refer them to the *Glossary* if necessary.

➕ Additional activity

(all levels)
If you have a number of CD players, divide the class into groups and give each group a player. Stronger students answer all questions. Weaker groups or individuals answer only selected questions from one or two parts. A student from each group reports back the answers to the class. Finally, play all parts to the whole class and check for understanding, pausing where necessary to discuss the correct answers.

➕ Additional activity

(stronger students)
Get students to organize these words and related forms in tables, continuing their word study from Unit 1: *evaluating, investigating, manufacturer, mass-produce*. (Possible answers: *evaluate / evaluation / evaluator; investigation / investigate / investigator; manufacture / manufacturing; mass-production / mass-producer*.)

4 Technology in sport

Background

Modern sports materials are subjected to powerful forces. When a racket hits a ball, the impact causes compression (= squeezing) and tension (= stretching), and may cause bending (= compression + tension). Repeated friction makes clothing wear (= erode) away. A bicycle pedal may break because of fatigue (= weakening) if it is turned the same way repeatedly.

Sports materials must have properties (= characteristics) to resist (= fight against) these forces. Equipment must be impact-resistant, fatigue-resistant, and tough (= difficult to break). Clothing must be wear-resistant, fit the body tightly and be aerodynamic (= able to move smoothly). Some materials should be rigid (= unbendable), others need to be flexible (= able to bend), or elastic (= able to change shape and return to their original shape). Some equipment must be hard (= able to cut, but not be cut by, other materials). For fast sports, equipment needs a high strength-to-weight ratio (combining strength with lightness).

Special materials are used for making modern sports equipment and clothing:

- **plastics** – these are light and can be moulded into shape. Examples: polycarbonate (goggles), polyurethane (footballs), and polystyrene (inside bike helmets)
- **fibres** – materials such as Lycra and Kevlar are used for sports clothing.
- **composites** – these combine fibres and plastic and have a good strength-to-weight ratio. Examples: fibreglass (boats), graphite, and carbon-fibre (bicycle frames)
- **laminates** – these are formed from two or more layers of plastic or composite metals such as titanium and aluminium, and alloys such as chrome-molybdenum (cro-moly) combine lightness, strength, and corrosion-resistance.

*Tip

Before you begin this unit, ask your students to bring some of their own sports equipment into class. You can then spend a few minutes before *Switch on* discussing the items and the materials they are made of as an introduction.

➕ Additional activities

(all levels)
Students describe to the whole class the items of sports equipment or clothing they have brought in (if you have not already done this). You can ask students to describe the items, the materials they are made of, and their properties.

(stronger students)
Students can ask each other questions about the items, and explain why certain properties are important for the specific sporting activities they are used for.

Switch on

Put students into small groups to do this task. Make sure they understand the words in the table. Explain or ask them to guess any unknown items. When they do the task, refer them to the *Glossary*. When they have finished the task, get someone from each group to give the group's answers. Ask stronger students to explain their reasons for matching components with materials and properties.

🔑
1 shoe soles   4 brake cables   7 frame
2 helmet   5 wheel bearings   8 saddle
3 tyres and pedals 6 rims

It's my job

1 Put students into pairs to discuss this question before looking at the text and to note down their ideas individually. Then let them read the text once and check their notes.

2 After students have finished reading individually, they can complete the table individually or in pairs. After the task, discuss the meanings of key terms such as *corrosion-resistant*, *strength-to-weight ratio*, and *elasticity*.

* Tip

yield strength – how much force you need to bend a material to a point where it can't return to its original shape

elongation strength – how much a material will bend or stretch before it breaks

* Tip

made of is normally used when only one material is mentioned and the material has not been processed or changed in any way.
made from is normally used when more than one material is mentioned, and / or the materials have been processed or changed in some way.

* Tip

BrE *fibre* AmE *fiber*
Fibreglass can also be written *fibre glass* and *fibre-glass*.
BrE *aluminium* AmE *aluminum*

Material	Advantages	Disadvantages
steel	not expensive, strong, good elasticity	heavy
aluminium	light, strong	flexible
titanium	good strength-to-weight ratio, corrosion-resistant	expensive
carbon fibre	very light, very strong, easy to shape	expensive

Language spot
used to, used for, made of, made from

Briefly discuss the differences between these structures. Refer to the *Grammar reference* on p.117. There is no difference in meaning or use between *Titanium is used **to make** the front fork* and *Titanium is used **for making** the front fork*. However, **made of** and **made from** are used differently (see *Tip*).

1 In pairs, students discuss the mistakes in the structures used in the sentences and correct them.

1 Rubber is used for making the tyres.
2 The frame is made of titanium.
3 Kevlar is used to make the rider's clothing.
4 Because it is very strong, braided steel is used to make brake cables.
5 Carbon fibre is used to make racing bike frames.
6 Steel is made from iron and carbon.

2 Students make sentences from the table on p.22.

1 The rider's shorts are made from Kevlar and nylon because they are wear-resistant.
2 The shoe soles are made of rubber because it provides a good grip.
3 The helmet is made from polystyrene and polycarbonate because they are strong and lightweight.
4 Rubber is used for the tyres and pedals because it provides a good grip.
5 Braided steel is used for making the brake cables because it is very strong.
6 Steel is used for making the wheel bearings because it is hard.
7 The rims are made of aluminium alloy because it is light and strong.
8 Titanium is used to make the frame because it is lighter and stronger than steel and highly corrosion-resistant.
9 The saddle is made of nylon because it is light and flexible.

3 Tell students to use their own knowledge to complete the table individually.

Possible answers
1 aluminium / wood (ash)
2 leather / polyurethane
3 fibreglass
4 aluminium / graphite / carbon-fibre
5 graphite composites
6 fibreglass / aluminium / plastic laminates
7 high carbon steel
8 plastic
9 steel / aluminium
10 aluminium and polyester

✱ Tip
Top margin
Discuss the statistic about the golf ball. Ask students if they can think of other sports where new technology has had a similar effect (graphite rackets in tennis, new spokes and frames in cycling).

✱ Tip
Opposites
tough ≠ brittle (= easy to break)
hard ≠ soft (= easy to cut into)
rigid ≠ flexible (= easy to bend)

Similar but different
elastic = able to change shape and able to return to its original shape
plastic = able to change shape, but unable to return to its original shape

➕ Additional activity
(stronger students)
Play a version of twenty questions dividing students into two teams, A and B. One student from Team A says he or she is thinking of a piece of sports equipment or clothing, without naming it. Students from Team B try to guess it by asking *Yes / No* questions only about property or materials used, e.g. *Is the material flexible? Does the material stretch and return to its original shape? Is it made from rubber and steel?* Check that they are using the correct intonation.

➕ Additional activity
(weaker students)
Play a simpler version of the twenty questions game in the previous activity. Limit the language to the following question types: *Can you bend it? Can you break it easily? Yes, you can. / No, you can't.* Limit the verbs to the following: *bend, stretch, break, cut, tear, burn*, and other similar verbs which they know. You can limit the objects to things in the classroom (such as *window, paper*) or to any everyday objects (such as *football, newspaper, water bottle*).

Pronunciation
Intonation for questions

1 🎧 Remind students of the difference between *wh-questions* (expecting information) and *Yes / No* questions (expecting only a *Yes* or *No* answer). Point out that these examples are *wh-questions*, and draw students' attention to the falling arrows that show the direction of the intonation.

2 🎧 Point out that these examples are *Yes / No* questions, and draw students' attention to the rising arrows.

3 🎧 Get students to mark the correct arrows on the emphasized word in the questions.

🔑 ⬇ (falling) ⬇ (falling) ⬆ (rising) ⬇ (falling)

4 Get students to work in pairs and ask questions about the table in *Language spot* **3**. Check that they are using the correct intonation.

Vocabulary
Describing materials

1 Before you set this task, refer back to the use of some of these terms in previous exercises. Tell students to check their work using the *Glossary*. Draw their attention to *tough* /tʌf/ and *toughness*. Point out that in *plastic* and *elastic* the final sound /k/ changes to /s/ when forming the nouns *plasticity* and *elasticity*.

🔑 2 plastic   6 brittleness
    3 strength   7 hard
    4 corrosion-resistant   8 toughness
    5 wear-resistance 9 flexible

2 Get students to do this individually. Encourage them to use the *Glossary* where necessary.

🔑 1 flexible   5 elastic
    2 corrosion-resistant   6 hard
    3 hard   7 brittle
    4 elasticity   8 wear-resistant

Gadget box

In small groups ask students to brainstorm as many ideas as they can to improve the gadget. When they have finished, ask one student from each group to present their ideas to the rest of the class. Get the whole class to vote on the best three improvements.

🔑 **Possible answer**
An LED display on the shoe could show distance or speed.

Speaking
Skateboard v snowboard

Check students understand the task: Student A labels the diagram and completes the table by asking Student B questions. Then Student B has to do the same by asking Student A. If one of a pair is weaker than the other, he / she should be Student B, who has less information to give.

Listening
Exchanging information

1 🎧 Get students to listen to the conversation and then repeat the activity in *Speaking*.

2 🎧 Get students to listen to the second part of the conversation again and fill the gaps.

🔑	1 made of	5 about, is it
	2 How come	6 When
	3 on both sides	7 are they
	4 it called	

Customer care
Making recommendations

1 Explain that the phrases in italics are different ways of recommending something. Get students to practise short phrases, e.g. *I'd go for a wooden deck*.

2 In pairs, tell the student making the recommendation to find out what the other student needs by asking a few questions first. For example, Student A asks *Do you want to skate in parks, streets, or on hills?* After getting information, Student A makes recommendations. For example: *You're quite tall, so your best bet for size is 60 mm. You want to do hills, so I'd go for 87A.*

Key words

Go through the list of words to check students' pronunciation and understanding. Refer them to the *Glossary* if necessary.

➕ Additional activity
(all levels)
Ask students to think of a sport or hobby that they know something about. Pair them with a 'beginner' and get them to make recommendations.

5 Appropriate technology

Background

Appropriate technology is technology which uses locally available materials and expertise to provide inexpensive solutions to problems in countries in the developing world, particularly in poorer rural areas. The wind pump is a typical example – it is relatively simple to construct and maintain, and does not require fuel. It contains a simple mechanism, a crankshaft, which converts the rotary (round and round) movement of the blades into a reciprocating (up and down) movement which, in turn, is linked to the piston of a pump.

The clockwork radio is a more sophisticated example. It consists of a clockwork motor which drives a small generator. This produces enough power to run the radio. The step-up gears increase the speed of rotation of the motor. The radio is cheap to use because it does not need **mains** power or batteries, which can be very expensive. The clockwork computer described in the Gadget box uses the same form of power. Its cost is kept low because the computer is not advertised, and it uses open-source software, which is available free to anyone (unlike Microsoft, for example, which requires users to pay for a licence).

Portable generators combine an engine, usually diesel, with an electric generator. They provide power in emergencies or in areas where no mains power is available, but are often very noisy. Noise is measured in decibels (dB) – the higher the number, the noisier the machine. At home, the generator may be used to power domestic appliances such as kettles, freezers, washing machines, and air conditioners. The amount of electricity they use is measured in kilowatts (kW). Lighting uses much less electricity.

Car engines are normally four-stroke. In a four-stroke petrol engine there is a cycle (or series) of events which is completed in four strokes (or movements) of the piston: on the induction stroke, the fuel is drawn into the cylinder, on the compression stroke, the fuel is compressed and ignited by the spark plug, on the power stroke, the piston is driven down the cylinder by the expanding gas from the burning fuel, and on the exhaust stroke, the rising piston pushes the exhaust gas out of the engine.

Two-stroke engines are used in portable devices such as chainsaws. They can be used at any angle. Put simply, in the two-stroke cycle, power and exhaust are combined in one stroke, compression and ignition in the other. There is no requirement for inlet and outlet valves for entry of the fuel or exit of the exhaust gas. This simplifies construction and reduces the cost of two-stroke engines. However, they are noisy and produce more pollution than four-stroke engines.

Switch on

1 Encourage students, working in pairs, to discuss the diagram freely for a short time, and then to answer the questions. Ask them to write down their answers briefly in note form.

2 Tell students to look at their own notes and make any changes necessary, as they listen.

> 1 A wind pump
> 2 It pumps water from under the ground.
> 3 The wind turns the blades. This rotary movement is converted into an up-and-down movement by a crankshaft connected to the piston of a pump.
> 4 In the developing world, for example, in India and Africa
> 5 Inexpensive materials

➕ Additional activity

(stronger students)
Select one or two students to come out to the front of the class and give a brief explanation in their own words (without looking at the reading text) of how the radio works.

✱ Tip

Ask students what kind of energy the wound spring has (*potential energy*). The machine converts potential energy into electrical energy.

✱ Tip

3V = 3 Volts
30 mA = 30 milli Amps (1 mA = 0.001 Amps)
Note the small *m* and the large *A*.

✱ Tip

Top margin
Closed source software is software owned by one company and sold to the public for profit. The source code (or program) is kept secret. The software may be too expensive for many people in developing countries. *Open source software* is produced by groups of computer specialists and given to the public free. The source code is made public. *Wi-Fi networks* allow computers to connect wirelessly (using radio signals) to the Internet. This is useful in areas of the developing world where there may be no cable infrastructure. *Wi-Fi* stands for *wireless fidelity*.

➕ Additional activity

(stronger students)
Ask one or two students to explain how they think the clockwork computer works (*it uses a similar mechanism to the clockwork radio*).

Reading
The inventor

1 Get students to cover the reading text (except for the photograph of the inventor) and discuss anything that they already know about the inventor. They should note down any points. If they need help, you can ask them why a clockwork radio might be useful in the developing world (*because it doesn't use expensive batteries or electricity*). Then get them to read the first paragraph and compare it with their notes.

2 Tell students to read the rest of the text individually and label the diagram. Encourage them to discuss the text with their partner if necessary. Afterwards, you can have a brief discussion with the whole class about how the device works.

🔑 1 c   2 e   3 d   4 b   5 a

3 Get students to do this exercise individually.

🔑 a clockwork radios in use all over the world
   b turns to wind up the spring fully
   c voltage of electricity generated
   d how long the radio will run
   e when Baylis heard about the problem of health information in Africa
   f electrical current generated

4 Get students to do this exercise individually.

🔑 1 you wind up a spring.   4 you have to wind it up again.
   2 the gears engage.   5 you walk.
   3 it generates electricity.

Gadget box

Put students into small groups of 3–5 to discuss the answers to the questions about the clockwork computer (see *Tip*).

Language spot
Time clauses

Refer students to the *Grammar reference* p.117 for a full explanation of the language points in this unit. Discuss the examples with the class. *When* shows a very close relationship between the two actions. The second action happens very quickly, almost immediately, after the first (often because the first action causes the second to happen). *Before* and *after* simply show the sequence of events, but there may be a long period of time between the two events. *As* is used when two actions take place at the same time.

1 Discuss the first three items with the class. In 1 and 2, different answers are possible. *When* is best in 1 to show that the blades have to turn before the piston moves. *As* is best in 2 to indicate that the rotation and the pumping happen at the same time. In 3, *after* is used to show the sequence of events. In 6, *when* suggests that she became an engineer immediately after leaving college.

1 When the wind turns the pump blades, the piston moves up and down.
2 As the blade rotates, water is pumped from the well.
3 After Baylis invented the clockwork radio, he invented the electric shoe.
4 The Internet existed before the World Wide Web became popular.
5 As the generator turns, it produces electricity.
6 When / After she left college, she became an engineer.
7 When / As you apply the brakes, the car slows down.
8 When / As you press the accelerator, the car speeds up.

2 Have a brief discussion with the class about how the two-stroke engine works. Then set the exercise. The exercise can be done either individually or in pairs, discussing the best answers.

| 1 Before | 3 As | 5 When | 7 before |
| 2 When | 4 As / When | 6 As | 8 after |

Problem-solving

1 If necessary, ask students which sentence comes first and discuss it if there is any difference of opinion. Then let them complete the task individually.

f a e d b c g

2 Get students to discuss the question in pairs.

d

3 Get students to discuss the question in pairs.

Possible answers
An efficient way of powering generators
Future cars
Powering moving machinery in space

Pairwork

1 Get students to discuss the question in pairs. They should be able to work out from the diagram and their general knowledge that the device uses the sun's rays to distill pure water from dirty water through evaporation.

2 Get students, in pairs, to ask each other questions until they understand how the device works, and can label their own diagram completely.

3 First get the pairs to discuss and agree how the device works. Then get them to listen to the recording. Ask them what new information (if any) they have learnt from the recording.

Speaking

1 Get students to do this individually.

2 Make sure students are using the *Useful language*.

Appropriate technology   25

Pronunciation
Numbers and quantities

1 🎧 For each item, get two or three students individually to read out the item. Then play the recording. Discuss any mistakes. Get the whole class (or small groups) to repeat the item correctly. Then move on to the next item.

2 🎧 Play all the items together and get students to write them down. Then play the items again and allow students to complete their work.

🔑
a -273.15 °C   e 1,048,576   i 13.5%
b 95.8 MHz   f 1:8   j 256 GB
c 110V AC   g 16 mm
d 2^{20} h 0.01

Refer students to the *Symbols and characters* table on p.114 for revision.

Vocabulary
Describing motion

1 Before they look at this exercise, ask students if they can remember any adjectives describing direction of motion from the reading texts in this unit. If they mention any words, such as *clockwise*, ask them to show with their hands what they mean. Then set the exercise.

🔑 1 F   2 E   3 C   4 D   5 B   6 A

2 Get students to test each other in pairs.

Customer care
Explaining the difference between products

Put students in pairs, Student A and Student B. The stronger student of the pair should be Student A (the Plant Hire Technician). Give them a little time to prepare their parts. Student B will mainly prepare questions, but also some answers based on their needs. Student A will have to prepare questions to find out what kind of generator the customer needs before recommending the best choice. When they have prepared their parts, get them to do the role-play.

Key words

Go through the list of words to check students' pronunciation and understanding. Refer them to the *Glossary* if necessary.

✱ Tip
BrE *anticlockwise*
AmE *counterclockwise*

➕ Additional activity
(weaker students)
Divide students into groups of around four. Write out a number of instructions on strips of paper, one instruction per strip. Make sure they are all simple practical actions which students can carry out. For example: *Move your hand in a rotary motion above your head. Move your left leg forwards and backwards.* Also write out the words *as, before,* and *after*, each word on a separate strip. Give about six instruction strips, and one each of the *as / before / after* strips to each member of the group. Each student in turn chooses another student and reads out a pair of instructions, joined with one of the sequence words. For example: *Move your hand in a rotary motion above your head – as – you move your left leg forwards and backwards.* The other student has to carry out the dual instruction.

✱ Tip
Point out that *pump* can be both noun and verb. Ask students to give an example of each. Point out that *charge* and *engage* (in the contexts given here) can be both transitive and intransitive. Examples: *He charged the battery (tr). The battery is charging (intr). The driver engaged first gear (tr). The gears engaged with a loud noise (intr).*

6 Crime-fighting and security

Background

Technology is becoming very important in crime-fighting and security. At the same time, criminals are finding new ways to use technology to commit crimes such as credit-card fraud (stealing money from other people's credit cards) and hacking (breaking into computer networks). The threat of terrorism has become greater in recent years. To combat this, devices have been developed to protect airports and other public places, and to check identities.

The pictures on p.34 show the equipment carried by a typical police officer in the UK. This special equipment provides protection against attack, and helps the officer to carry out his or her duties. Handcuffs are used to restrain offenders (prevent them from moving). Firearms or guns are not normally carried in the UK. Instead police are armed with non-lethal (non-deadly) weapons such as an extendable baton. This is manufactured from polycarbonate which can be used to produce very strong mouldings. Police may also use CS gas to incapacitate (or weaken) violent offenders. Some police forces are experimenting with taser guns which fire a dart attached to electrical wires. Tasers deliver a high voltage but low current shock to the offender, which causes temporary paralysis but does not cause long-term harm.

Personal Identification Numbers (PIN) in combination with electronic chips inserted in credit cards (chip and PIN) have reduced card fraud. Global Positioning Systems (GPS), which can accurately identify a location to within a few metres using signals from earth-orbiting satellites, can be used to monitor the movement of a tag fastened to an offender's leg. This is much cheaper than sending people to prison for certain offences.

Other crime prevention measures include the use of remote **sensors** which can detect or measure changes in the environment, such as motion, shock, smoke, etc. High resolution cameras, like Flashcam, can be used to monitor an area continually. If the picture changes, the sensor (in this case a camera) triggers an alarm. The cameras can be rotated (turned) and tilted (moved upwards and downwards) by an operator, sometimes many kilometres away, using radio signals, so that a complete check of the surroundings can be made.

The science of **biometrics**, the ability to identify the individual by some unique property such as voice or face, is behind the development of iris scanning (which recognizes someone's eyes) and dynamic grip recognition (which recognizes the shape of a gun-owner's hand). Iris scanning is used to identify frequent-flying passengers on airlines to speed up their passage through security controls. The USA has introduced biometric passports to guard against identity fraud (the crime of stealing another person's identity).

Robots are used in security because they can perform tasks either more cheaply or without risk to human life. They are programmed to perform an activity when they receive a signal. The signal may come from sensors inside or outside the robot. In the case of Rotundus, the sensors (cameras, microphones, heat detectors, and smoke detectors) are all internal.

Switch on

Ask students to attempt to name items of the police officer's equipment from their general knowledge.

○┳ torch, handcuffs, baton, radio, CS gas canister, knife vest

*Tip

Low-tech (low technology) refers to older, simpler technology such as torches, handcuffs, batons, guards, and dogs. *Hi-tech* (high technology) refers to newer, more complex technology often using electronics, such as tasers.

Listening

Crime-fighting equipment

1 🎧 Play the recording once without pausing, while students complete column A. Discuss their answers and check that they have the correct items of equipment before doing the next exercise.

Crime-fighting and security 27

2 🎧 Play the recording again while students complete column B.

A Item	B Function
handcuffs	restrain someone
baton	keep people at a safe distance
CS gas	incapacitate a violent person
knife-proof vests	body armour
taser	give a powerful electric shock
radio	contact each other and police headquarters
notebook	–

* Tip

restrain means to tie someone up (with rope or handcuffs) so that they cannot move
incapacitate means to make someone unable to do anything dangerous, for example by spraying with gas or firing a stun gun. This should not kill or permanently injure the person.

➕ Additional activity

(weaker students)
In small groups of 4–6, students make a small pile of objects on a desk in the middle of the group. They should put as many things as they can find, such as protractors, rulers, pencil cases, etc. Try to bring some unusual objects into class, and give a few to each group. Then get students to take turns to pick up any object and ask its function (using a range of forms): *What's this for? What's this used as? What's this used for?* with other students taking turns to try to answer.

* Tip

The words *waterproof* and *foolproof* are normally written without hyphens, because they are so commonly used. Most other words ending in *–proof* can be written with or without a hyphen.
There is a slight difference in degree between *waterproof* and *water-resistant*, where *–proof* is more effective than *–resistant*. But in most contexts they mean essentially the same thing.

Language spot
Describing function

Refer to the *Grammar reference* p.118 for a full explanation of the language points in this unit. Discuss the examples with the class. Correct students who omit *is* or *are* in expressions such as *handcuffs are used to restrain someone* and *a taser is used to stun someone*. The form *used as* + noun is commonly used when the noun (expressing the function) is slightly unexpected. For example, you expect a belt to be used *for wearing*, but sometimes it is unexpectedly used *as a weapon*.

1 Get students to do this exercise individually. Check that they have the correct answers before doing the next exercise.

2 g   3 h   4 e   5 f   6 i   7 d   8 a   9 j   10 c

2 Encourage pairs to vary the language forms they use in both question and answer.

Vocabulary
-proof, -resistant, -tight

1 Discuss the examples with students.

2 Different wordings are possible. Point out that some of the items are in the plural, so that students will have to use the plural forms, for example (in 5) *aren't damaged by* instead of *isn't damaged by*.

1 a seal which gas can't pass through
2 paint which isn't damaged by weather
3 materials which aren't damaged by heat
4 a recording studio which is protected from (external) sounds
5 car bodies which aren't damaged by rust
6 a device which can't be damaged by fools (i.e. is easy to use)
7 a coat which water can't pass through easily
8 a container which water can't pass through

➕ Additional activity

(all students)

Ask students what rules their country has made about having their passport photograph taken. Get them to read the information at the top of the page. These rules are designed to allow face-recognition security devices to work properly.

✱ Tip

Top margin

Ask students if they know any other rules about passport photos. For example, *not wearing a hat*, etc.

➕ Additional activity

(stronger students)

Ask stronger students from two groups with different solutions to hold a short debate in front of the class. Encourage them to give a fuller account of their decision, going through the reasons for accepting / rejecting each device, and adding some reasons of their own.

Pairwork

1 Tell the pairs to discuss the titles without looking at the texts.

2 Get each student to read their own text. When they have finished reading, get them to find out about the other student's device by asking the questions and noting down the answers.

> **Student A**
> 1 Smart gun (dynamic grip recognition)
> 2 It stops anyone firing a gun who is not the owner of the gun.
> 3 The handle of the gun is fitted with sensors which measure grip pressure. The pressure is then compared with the owner's.
> 4 In New Jersey
> 5 Early results show that it works.
>
> **Student B**
> 1 Flashcam
> 2 It gives warnings and takes pictures in areas with crime problems.
> 3 It's fitted with a motion sensor.
> 4 In areas which have a crime problem
> 5 It has had a positive effect in some parts of London.

3 When students have finished, get them to read each other's text and check the information they have noted down.

4 Let students remain in pairs for a few minutes to discuss these questions. Then bring the class together for a short class discussion.

Problem-solving

In small groups, get students to discuss this problem and agree on the best solution. Tell them they have to give reasons for their decision. Before they start discussing, get each group to appoint a chairperson to lead the discussion and a reporter who will note down all their decisions. When they have finished, get each group to tell the rest of the class their decision.

Gadget box

Discuss *Rotundus* with the whole class. Check that they understand the meaning of a *sensor*. This is a device which sends a signal when it detects changes in the environment. Ask them how an intruder can escape from the device (one answer: *by running up or down stairs*). Advantages of *Rotundus* over human and animal guards: *it is small and can follow intruders without being seen or heard; it can follow them over all types of surface; and it cannot be injured, bribed, drugged, poisoned, or killed.*

Crime-fighting and security

*Tip

Although

although = in spite of the fact that
1 *Although* these cameras deter thieves, the image may not be clear.
2 These cameras deter thieves *although* the image may not be clear.

Example 1 emphasizes the disadvantage.
Example 2 emphasizes the advantage.

Writing
Short report and linking words

1 First discuss the language points and examples provided. Point out the different uses of *however* and *although*. *However* introduces a whole sentence which contrasts with the previous sentence. *Although* contrasts one clause or part of a sentence with another part of the same sentence.

2 Discuss the writing with the whole class. Tell them to use the material in *Problem-solving*. Set this as individual work. Weaker students can work in pairs and take responsibility for writing a shorter part of a joint report.

Customer care
Using informal language

1 Get students to read about the three home security systems quickly and silently. Then get them to note down some advantages and disadvantages of each system.

2 Explain the task. Tell students to work in pairs, with one student taking the part of the salesperson and the other the part of a customer who wants to buy a home security system. Before they begin, discuss the language in the boxes. The top row is more formal, and the second row is less formal. Practise these phrases with students. Then explain that the salesperson has to use the appropriate level of formality or informality depending on how formal or informal the customer appears to be. Bring a pair of stronger students to the front of the class and get them to perform the role-play. Treat the customer's level of formality / informality with tact and humour.

Key words

Go through the list of words to check students' pronunciation and understanding. Refer them to the *Glossary* if necessary. Check that they remember what *GPS (Global Positioning System)* and *PIN (Personal Identification Number)* stand for. Remind them that the noun related to *(electronic) tagging* is *(electronic) tag*. The word *trigger* can be a noun *(the trigger of a gun)* and a verb *(the sensor triggers an alarm)*.

7 Manufacturing

Background

Manufacturing means changing raw materials into products using a range of processes. For example, in bread manufacturing, you start with the raw materials: flour, water, yeast, and fat. These materials are changed into a final **product**: a loaf of bread wrapped in plastic foil. They are changed into the product by a number of *processes* or actions: for example mixing, cutting, putting into tins, baking, cooling, taking out of tins, spraying, slicing, and wrapping.

In the past, these processes were mainly done manually (by hand), but now manufacturers want to keep costs low, avoid waste, and make high-quality products as quickly as possible. Increasingly these jobs are done by using computer-controlled automation. Food processing is an important area of automated technology. The bread-making factory in this unit has more in common with a car assembly plant or with steel-making than with a traditional bakery where bread was made by hand. (*Assembly* means fixing together parts which have already been produced.) The factory runs for 24 hours a day and very little is done by hand. The work force is small so costs are low. A lot of **mass-produced** food and drink comes from factories like this.

Every type of manufacturing has its own special processes. An illustrated list of some of the most common processes is provided in the Reading bank (pp.56–58) of the Student's Book. In metal manufacturing, impact extrusion is a process by which a sheet of metal is pushed or drawn up into shape. Aluminium cans are made in this way. Bonding is joining materials using adhesives. Welding joins metals by heating them to melting point. Plating is applying a thin layer or coat of metal to another metal to improve its appearance or to protect it from corrosion.

In plastics manufacturing, injection moulding is a common way of making plastic items such as bottle tops, caps, and CD covers. The hopper is a container or reservoir which feeds pellets (small pieces) of plastic into the barrel of the machine. The ram is like a piston. It pushes the soft warm plastic along the barrel into the mould. The mould is usually water-cooled to allow the molten plastic to set quickly.

∗ Tip

a *process* is a sequence of actions which changes materials or assembles parts into a completed product
a *product* is a completed, finished item which can be sold

∗ Tip

extrusion (n) is related to the verb *extrude*, which means to push (or squeeze) a substance out of a container. When you squeeze a toothpaste tube, you extrude the toothpaste.
injection (n) is the opposite process, related to the verb *inject*, which means to push a substance into a container. Doctors and nurses inject medicines into a patient's arm.

Switch on

1 Ask the class what they think is meant by a *manufacturing process*. Ask them the difference between a *process* and a *product*. Ask them what would be a good heading for the column with pictures (*Product*). Get them to write materials from the list in the centre column. Discuss their answers.

2 Discuss students' answers, then get them to write processes from the list in the right-hand column. Discuss their answers.

Answers for 1 and 2

	Materials	Processes
drinks can	*aluminium alloy*	*colour-printing, impact extrusion*
mountain bike	*steel, titanium, rubber*	*cutting, bending, moulding, welding, painting, assembly*
CD cases	*plastic*	*injection moulding*

It's my job

1 This activity prepares students for the listening activity which follows. In pairs, get students to answer as much as possible from their general knowledge. Each student should note down his / her own answers to the questions.

✱ Tip

To *prove* dough is to give enough time to allow the yeast to form small air bubbles in the dough. This takes place in the *prover*.

2 🎧 Play the recording without pauses and get individuals to check their own answers, noting down changes as necessary.

> 1 making and mixing dough, cutting into loaves, putting into tins, waiting for yeast to work in prover, baking, cooling, taking out of tins, spraying with chemical, slicing, wrapping
> 2 Manufacturing Engineer
> 3 a weight of ingredients, b mixing, c in prover, d baking, e cooling, f loaves made per hour, g loaves made per day

3 🎧 Play the recording again, and get individuals to complete the table.

> 1 the ingredients are mixed, 3 the loaves are baked,
> 5 the loaves are sprayed with a chemical, 6 the loaves are sliced,
> 7 the loaves are wrapped and sent to the supermarkets

Language spot
Present Passive

Refer students back to the table in the previous exercise with all the stages of the breadmaking process. Elicit the form of the verb used in each box (*Passive form*, *Present Simple*, and / or *Present Passive*). Take one of the sentences and show how it relates to the Active form: *(something) mixes the ingredients* → *the ingredients are mixed*. Explain that the Passive is used in descriptions of processes because the focus of attention is on the *action*, not on the thing or person doing the action.

Read through the explanation of the Present Passive in the Student's Book, and discuss it with students. Notice that the questions *Where? Why?* and *How?* are only answered where necessary. In the examples given, the reader probably needs to know the information contained in the words *in a steel mixer*, *to make dough*, and *by using suction*, because it is not obvious from the context.

1 Check students' understanding by doing item 1 together. Ask them why they think the Passive form is used, and ask them why they think no information is given to the *How?* question (*probably because mixing is an obvious action*).

> 1 in a steel mixer; to make dough
> 2 in a prover
> 3 in giant gas ovens
> 4 using suction
> 5 to keep them fresh longer
> 6 in a high-speed slicer; with giant saw blades
> 7 by the wrapping machine

✚ Additional activity
(weaker students)
Give students more practice in use of the Passive using simple vocabulary. In small groups each group thinks of a simple, everyday process that has no more than five or six steps, all done by hand. Tell the group to come up with sentences consisting of *You + verb + object*. For example: To fry an egg: *1 You heat the pan. 2 You pour the oil. 3 You break an egg. 4 You fry the egg. 5 You serve the egg.* Check the group's work. Try to get them to avoid phrasal verbs (e.g. use *pour the oil* instead of *put in the oil*). When they have a set of sentences, tell each student individually to write the process in the Passive, omitting the subject *you*. Example: *1 The pan is heated. 2 The oil is poured. 3 An egg is broken. 4 The egg is fried. 5 The egg is served.*

2 Get students to write a sentence for each stage in the form of a simple paragraph based on the above information. Tell them to use a variety of sequence words (*first, then, next, after*, etc.).

> Then the dough is cut into loaves, put into tins, and left in a prover for the yeast to work.
> After that, the loaves are baked in giant gas ovens.
> Next, the loaves are left to cool; then taken out of their tins by using suction.
> Then the loaves are sprayed with a chemical to keep them fresh longer.
> After that, the loaves are sliced in a high-speed slicer with giant saw blades.
> Finally, the loaves are wrapped and sent to the supermarkets.

32　Unit 7

✶Tip

Ask students what shape they think the *hopper* is. It looks triangular in the 2-D diagram, but it's *cone*-shaped, like a funnel. The pieces of raw plastic are poured into it, collected there until needed, and then passed (or *fed*) through it into the barrel.

✶Tip

Top margin

Ask students to research other products and the companies that are the largest manufacturers of these products. When they have a list of five or six, put them in pairs to quiz their partners.

Writing
Short sequence

1 Discuss the diagram of the injection moulding machine with the class. Get one or two stronger students to explain very briefly in their own words how it works (without reading the exercise). Now get them to do the task individually.

> 1 　　The hopper is filled with plastic.
> 2e　 The plastic is fed into the barrel.
> 3a　 The plastic is carried through the barrel by the rotating screw.
> 4d　 The plastic travels through the barrel.
> 5c　 The plastic is melted by the heaters.
> 6f　 There is enough melted plastic in the barrel.
> 7i　 The screw is pushed forward by the ram.
> 8b　 The hot plastic is injected quickly into the mould.
> 9h　 The plastic is left to set before the pressure is removed.
> 10g　The mould is cool.
> 11　 The finished moulding is removed.

2 Remind students of the time words: *when, as, before, after*. Get them to combine pairs of sentences into longer sentences.

> d + c　As the plastic travels through the barrel, it is melted by the heaters.
> f + i　When there is enough melted plastic in the barrel, the screw is pushed forward by the ram.
> g + 11　When the mould is cool, the finished moulding is removed.

Pairwork

1 In pairs, get students to study the diagram together and discuss how CDs are made.

2 Ask students to look at their short texts. Working individually, A and B match their short texts to stages on the diagram.

3 Get A and B to discuss their information with each other and agree on the correct order for all of the texts.

> 1 B　2 E　3 A　4 D　5 C　6 F

Speaking

1 Most food and drink products these days are manufactured on a large scale, so students can name almost any food or drink.

2 Encourage students to choose the food or drink they know most about.

3 Encourage students to collaborate as much as possible, using the *Useful language* to make suggestions.

4 Make sure that all students in each group have given an explanation of a process each.

Reading
Modern manufacturing processes

1 In groups of three, get each student to read a different text, then tell the rest of the group how their process works, its advantages, and examples of its use.

2 Get students to work individually and complete the table for the three texts.

Process	Advantages	Example of use
Electroforming	can make very fine components with precise dimensions	CDs
Water jet abrasive cutting	can cut almost any kind of material and doesn't change the properties of the materials it cuts	surgery
Hydroforming	fewer operations to produce complicated parts	low weight, high strength car body parts

Vocabulary
Compound nouns

Point out that the first noun in a compound is never plural, e.g. *bodies of cars* becomes *car bodies*.

1 covers of computers
2 forming by vacuum
3 pipes made of pvc
4 wings of planes
5 mixer made of steel
6 pump which uses wind
7 bearings made of steel
8 radio which uses clockwork

Webquest

Get students to do this exercise individually or in small groups.

Possible answers
1 stamping, welding
2 injection moulding
3 stamping, riveting, assembly
4 vacuum forming
5 extrusion

Key words

Go through the list of words to check students' pronunciation and understanding. Refer them to the *Glossary* if necessary.

⊕ Additional activity
(stronger students)
Get students to make a list of all the processes mentioned in this and earlier units, and make a table, showing related verbs and process nouns, like this

Verb	Process noun
bond	bonding
extrude	extrusion
plate	plating
weld	welding
cool	cooling

8 Transport

Background

Transport technology is concerned with all types of transport as well as roads, railways, airports, and sea ports. Engineers are involved in transport at all levels, from how to make fuels more efficient to designing longer and stronger bridges.

A major challenge for engineers is to design safer vehicles. Advanced Safety Vehicles use sensors to provide information to an onboard computer on all possible dangers. The sensors can detect obstacles near the car, such as other cars, pedestrians, or walls; they can detect changes in temperature, speed, acceleration, tyre pressure, and road surface. They can also sense changes in the driver's condition, such as eye blinking through tiredness. The sensors send a signal to the computer, which is programmed to take certain actions. For example, if a tyre suddenly loses pressure, or the car is too close to another vehicle, the computer sounds an alarm. The computer can take control of the car if necessary, and can cut the engine or apply the brakes.

Engineers are also attempting to design cars which run on 'ecologically friendly' fuels, rather than petrol or diesel. **Hybrid** (mixed) cars combine the internal combustion engine and the electric motor. The aim is to reduce fuel consumption and exhaust emissions by switching between the two power sources or combining the two to match the kind of driving required at any time. For example, when the car is moving slowly in a traffic jam it can switch to electricity, and when acceleration is required it can switch back to petrol again. Hybrid cars also have a wider range: they can travel 30% further than conventional cars on the same amount of fuel.

Hydrogen fuel cells use the world's most common element to generate electricity. Hydrogen stored under pressure is combined with oxygen pumped from outside the car. The chemical energy generated by this reaction is converted into electrical energy to power electric motors. The only by-product is steam. This means that it is an ecologically clean fuel, which can reduce emissions of greenhouse gases. But unfortunately it has some disadvantages at present: the fuel cells are expensive to manufacture, energy is consumed producing pure hydrogen, and it may be dangerous to store such an explosive gas in city centres.

City authorities are increasingly concerned at the poor quality of air in city streets because of vehicle exhausts. LPG (liquefied petroleum gas) produces 50% less pollution than the average diesel vehicle. Biogas or methane, from human or animal waste, can be collected and processed to fire electricity generating stations. In some countries, particularly Brazil, biofuels are produced from sugar cane or maize as an additive to diesel.

*Tip

- The **bullet train** (or **shinkansen**) links Tokyo with southern cities, travelling at speeds over 300 km/h.
- The Australian **road train** is a powerful truck with a number of trailers attached.
- The **solar-powered car** is an experimental prototype. It has a large surface area covered in **solar panels**, which absorb maximum energy from the sun. It is also made as light as possible to minimize the power required to drive it.
- The **space shuttle** can only be transported in this way in good weather conditions, and needs another plane to fly ahead to warn of changing weather.

Switch on

1 Get students to identify the forms of transport, and have a brief discussion about some of their interesting features.

> A bullet train
> B (Australian) road train
> C helicopter
> D American space shuttle on its carrier
> E solar-powered car
> F oil-tanker

2 In small groups, get students to brainstorm a list of other types of transport, grouped under the headings: land, sea, and air. Then briefly get each group to report back to the whole class.

> **Possible answers**
> land: bike, bus, motorbike, van
> sea: hovercraft, motor boat, sailing ship
> air: airbus, airship, glider

Transport 35

Reading
The car of the future

1 Before students look at the reading text, get them to study the diagram and discuss the four questions in pairs and note down their answers.

> 1 It is much safer.
> 2 Advanced Safety Vehicle
> 3 To protect the driver and other road users
> 4 **Possible answer** Sensor to detect road temperature in case of ice

2 After they have read the text, get students to check their answers to the pre-reading questions in **1**.

3 Get students to do this exercise individually, and then compare their answers in pairs.

	Advantages	Disadvantages
electric	efficient, no pollution	heavy batteries, limited range
hybrid (petrol and electric)	save about 15% of fuel, batteries don't have to be charged overnight	need batteries
LPG	cars can be converted easily	only cuts down pollution a little
hydrogen fuel cell	provide clean power	each cell is very expensive

Gadget box

Discuss this with the whole class and encourage humorous suggestions (*attaching a sound system which plays the sound of a motorbike engine*).

It's my job

1 🎧 Play the recording once and get students to note down as many answers as possible. Play the recording again and get them to complete the exercise.

> 1 Natural gas-fuelled buses
> 2 It improves air quality.
> 3 Gas-powered generators
> 4 Biogas
> 5 His company is planning to export to other EU countries.

Language spot
Prediction: *will, may, might*

Refer to the information in the *Grammar reference* p.119. Discuss the use of *will*, *may*, and *might*. Point out that the short forms *won't* and *mightn't* are not used in formal, written English.

1 Get students to do this exercise individually.

> 1 won't   5 will
> 2 will   6 may / might
> 3 may / might 7 will
> 4 won't   8 may / might

✱ Tip

hybrid = mixed. A hybrid car engine combines a petrol engine with some other type of engine, such as electric or hydrogen
range = the distance a car can travel on a full tank of fuel

2 Get students to write five simple predictions using *will*, *may*, or *might*, or their negatives. When they have finished, get them to work in pairs and discuss their predictions until they agree on the same predictions. Then select a few pairs and ask them to read out their predictions to the class.

Pronunciation

Corrective stress

1 🎧 Play the example, and ask students to tell you which word is stressed in the second statement (*are*). Ask them why they think this word is stressed (*because it expresses the disagreement*).

2 Get students to correct the statements individually in preparation for the next exercise. They can simply cross out the wrong word and write the correct word in.

> 1 No, hybrid cars have a *petrol* engine and an electric motor.
> 2 No, hydrogen fuel cells *aren't* cheap / *are* expensive.
> 3 No, most car drivers *aren't* happy / *are* unhappy to use public transport.
> 4 No, LPG cuts down pollution a *little*.
> 5 No, ASVs are *safer* for pedestrians.
> 6 No, solar power *isn't* the answer to our transport problems.
> 7 No, air travel *isn't* good / *is* bad for the environment.
> 8 No, trains and *buses* are examples of public transport.

3 Get one student to read out a statement, and another student to contradict the statement. Make sure that the second student stresses only the word expressing the disagreement.

4 🎧 Get students to listen and practise where necessary.

5 In pairs, get one student to choose a topic and make a statement about it, expressing an opinion. The other disagrees and makes a contrasting statement (with reasons for disagreement). Walk around the pairs and check that they are using corrective stress as in the previous exercises.

➕ Additional activity

(weaker students)
In groups, each student in the group writes down two or three simple predictions about sport, the next Olympics, space travel, inventions, or some other topic that interests them. Check that their sentences are short and simple, for example: *I think England will win the next World Cup*. Then get each student to say his / her predictions, and another student to disagree and make a new prediction about the same topic. (Remind them to stress the new word, in italics below.) Example:
A I think England will win the World Cup.
B I disagree. England *won't* win the World Cup. I think *Greece* will win it.

Problem-solving

1 Get students to discuss this in pairs.

> A microlite
> B aquatic car
> C Segway human transporter
> D Mars explorer
> E quad bike

2 Get students to continue discussing in pairs.

> **Possible answers**
> microlite   Must be lightweight, strong, aerodynamic
> aquatic car   Must be water-tight, buoyant, able to transfer power from wheels to a propeller, able to steer in water
> Segway   Must be able to remain upright
> Mars explorer Must be able to operate remotely in extreme conditions
> quad bike   Must be able to operate safely in off-road conditions

*Tip

Top margin
Compare the JCB with other land speed records:
Solar powered car – 48.71 mph (1988)
Bicycle – 167.043 mph (1995)
Electric car – 245.523 mph
Land car – 763.055 mph
If students want speeds in kph tell them an easy way for a rough conversion is to divide by five and multiply by eight.

Customer care
Making and acknowledging apologies

Discuss the importance of apologizing to customers and explain that it is also important to acknowledge apologies. Get students to practise the phrases and discuss the examples of written apologies.

Get students in pairs to practise apologizing and acknowledging, using the situations. Remind the first speaker in each dialogue to explain the situation first. They can also suggest some situations from their own technical field and then practise more apologies and acknowledgements.

Vocabulary
Recording new expressions

1 Remind students about grouping new vocabulary by *subjects* (Unit 1). Explain that it is also useful to group expressions by *function*.

2 Get students to complete the table.

Function	Expression
Opening a letter or email	Hi …
	Dear …
Closing a letter or email	Regards …
	Best wishes …
Referring to previous contact	I wrote to you on (date) …
	We spoke (last week) …
Giving reasons	I'm writing to you because …
	The reason I'm getting in touch is …
Promising action	We will …
	We're going to …
	I can assure you that …

+ Additional activity
(stronger students)
When they have written their email, get stronger students in pairs to role play a telephone call in which they play the parts of the customer and the person writing the email.
- The email writer phones the customer two days later to check if he / she received the last air-conditioning unit.
- The customer says he / she has received it. The writer then apologizes again for the delay.
- The customer acknowledges the apology and thanks the writer for making sure that the problem was resolved so quickly.

3 Get students to write the email, using some of the phrases practised and discussed. Check their work individually.

Possible answer
Dear Mr / Ms X,
The reason I'm getting in touch is to apologize for sending you the wrong number of air-conditioning units. We *very much regret* the mistake in your order. *We spoke yesterday* and I have found out the reason for the error. This was due to the fact that we only had the five units in stock. *We will* receive a new batch tomorrow and *I can assure you* that the remaining unit will be sent by express delivery.
Regards,

Webquest

Students can work in small groups or pairs to do this research.

Key words

Go through the list of words to check students' pronunciation and understanding. Refer them to the *Glossary* if necessary.

9 High living: skyscrapers

Background

High buildings, often called skyscrapers, allow us to make maximum use of the limited and often expensive building land in cities. They can also demonstrate the confidence and importance of a company, city, or country, and lead to never-ending competition to build the highest tower.

When we look at a skyscraper, we see the shining metal or glass exterior. But this is only the outer covering. All the load-bearing structure is inside the building. A high building is like a human or animal body: it consists of a structural **skeleton** inside and an outer **skin** or covering. The structural skeleton of the skyscraper is made of steel and consists of vertical columns, horizontal girders, and (sometimes) diagonal braces to give extra strength. These are all made of steel beams (long narrow bars), which are joined together using bolts and rivets. To make the girders more rigid and prevent them from buckling (or bending), they are often made with a cross-section in the shape of the letter *I* (I-shaped girders).

When the columns and girders for one **storey** or level are in position, the concrete floor is made. This is done by laying metal decking (flat metal sheets like the deck of a boat) across the girders and filling them with liquid concrete. The decking acts as a former, which forms or moulds the concrete to the correct shape. Ducts (long narrow containers) are placed under the floors to carry the cables and pipes of the electrical and plumbing services. Most high buildings are constructed using the process of prefabrication, in which complete sections or floors are fabricated (built) beforehand at ground level, then lifted by cranes and fitted into position.

When the steel structure is completed, the outside of the building is covered with its outer skin, called the cladding, or curtain wall. This consists of panels made of a variety of materials, such as glass, aluminium, or stainless steel.

Skyscrapers impose a massively concentrated load on their **foundations**. Where poor ground conditions exist, huge effort is put into creating suitable foundations through the use of piles and concrete rafts. Piles are long columns made from steel or reinforced concrete. Steel piles are driven vertically into the ground by a piledriver until they reach bedrock (a layer of rock deep in the ground) or a stable layer of heavy clay which is considered suitable to bear the weight of the building. Reinforced concrete piles are made by drilling to the correct depth, inserting a network of steel rods, then filling the hole with concrete. A concrete raft is a flat base or platform of steel-reinforced concrete, which is formed above the piles and attached to them. This spreads the weight of the building over a wide area and through the piles to the bedrock. Another way of spreading weight is by using thick bases called piers which are splayed (or expanded outwards) like small pyramids.

In earthquake zones, special foundations are constructed which permit the tower to rock backwards and forwards, and absorb the force of the shock without serious damage. In windy conditions, a skyscraper will sway by as much as fifteen centimetres.

∗ Tip

Some famous skyscrapers and their cities:
Taipei 101, Taipei
Petronas Towers, Kuala Lumpur
Sears Tower, Chicago
Jin Mao Tower, Shanghai

Switch on

1 Do this activity with the whole class. Get students to brainstorm the names of famous skyscrapers and their cities.

2 Discuss the diagram with the whole class, then get students to discuss in pairs and note down as many words as they can from their general knowledge.

🔑 1 e 2 d 3 b 4 c 5 a 6 f

High living: skyscrapers   39

It's my job

1 🎧 Play the recording and get students to note down the answers individually.

> 1 four guys, including Leon
> 2 a few weeks to a year
> 3 supermarkets, warehouses, and multi-storey buildings
> 4 prefabricated
> 5 twelve hours

2 🎧 Play the recording again and get students to note down the answers individually.

> 1 It depends on the size of the building.
> 2 For finishing ahead of schedule.
> 3 To make sure everything reaches you in the right order.
> 4 It's too much time and effort to make the journey and everything you need is up top.
> 5 They can crush you.

Reading
How skyscrapers are built

1 First get students to write their answers individually without looking at the text. Then, in small groups get them to compare their answers. Do not check or correct their answers at this point.

> a 4   b 7   c 3   d 1   e 5   f 6   g 2   h 8

2 Get students to read the text and check their answers.

Language spot
Safety signs and safety advice

Get students to tell you the meaning of any of the signs in the photo. Then get them to brainstorm other safety signs they might see on a building site. They can come out and draw the signs on the board.

Point out the different ways of expressing safety instructions: *No -ing*, *Do not …*, *You must not …*, *Wear …*, *… must be worn*. Refer to the *Grammar reference* p.119 for further information.

1 Get students to match signs and meanings individually.

> 1 d   2 c   3 b   4 a   5 f   6 e

2 In pairs, get students to take turns: one student is a trainee and the other student is an experienced worker explaining to the trainee what the signs mean. The worker first gives the formal meaning, from **1**, then explains it in simpler language, as in the example.

3 Get students to do this task individually.

---

* **Tip**

columns are vertical
girders are horizontal
braces are diagonal
ducts are long hollow containers for holding wires and pipes
piles are steel or concrete vertical foundations

* **Tip**

storey = floor
In Britain and most of Europe the storey at the ground level is called the *ground floor*, and the floor above is the *first floor*.
In the USA, Russia, and some eastern European countries, the floor at the ground level is usually called the *first floor*, and the floor above is the *second floor*.

* **Tip**

Top margin
Compare the Home Insurance building with the Sears Tower, now the tallest building in Chicago, which has 108 storeys and was completed in 1973.

> **O**⚷ **Possible answers**
> 1 Always make sure a machine has stopped before removing the guards.
> 2 Never use mobile phones in busy working areas.
> 3 Always wear eye protection when using grinders.
> 4 Never smoke near flammable substances.
> 5 Always wear a hard hat when work is going on overhead.
> 6 Never operate chain saws without ear protection.
> 7 Always make sure the mains supply is disconnected before working on electrical equipment.
> 8 Always store chemicals in a lockable room or container.

Customer care

Showing visitors round a construction site

1 Get students to work in pairs. After their discussion they can make a list of safety rules which they think the people in the picture are breaking.

2 Get students to work individually, using the text and their own general knowledge. Weaker students can work in pairs.

> **O**⚷ | **Regulation** | **Reason** |
> |---|---|
> | Make sure the hard hat fits. | It's useless and dangerous if it falls off. |
> | Wear boots. | There may be nails or spills anywhere. |
> | Don't carry loose papers. | He doesn't want papers blowing round the site. They may cause accidents. |
> | No flash photography on the floor levels. | It can distract. |
> | Don't pick anything up. | It might cut or burn. |
> | Keep with the group. | You might be left behind or get into a dangerous situation. |
> | Look out for forklifts. | Forklifts aren't looking out for pedestrians. |

Pronunciation

Stress in long words (1)

1 Explain to students that hearing the stress on the correct syllable in a long word is very important to understanding meaning. Check that they understand the meaning of *syllable*.

🎧 Do the first two or three words with the whole class before they do the exercise individually.

> **O**⚷ b 3 c 3 d 3 e 2 f 2 g 3 h 5 i 3 j 3 k 4 l 5

Check that students can hear which syllable is stressed in the words in **1**. Play the words from **1** again and get individual students to tap out the syllables on the desk, stressing the correct syllable with a louder tap.

2 In pairs, get students to compare how they think the syllables are stressed and complete the table. Do not check their answers yet.

➕ Additional activity
(all levels)
In small groups, students brainstorm a list of items of safety clothing or equipment (*safety helmet / hard hat, safety goggles, safety boots, ear muffs, safety harness, lifeline*). Get them to compile a list of safety instructions using the same structures, for example: *Always wear / use (safety goggles) in / on the (workshop).* Get stronger students to use this structure: *(Hard hats) must always be worn / used in / on the (building site).*

➕ Additional activity
(weaker students)
In small groups, students brainstorm a list of items or activities which must be avoided (*smoking, mobile phones, running, eating, shouting, diving*). Get them to compile a list of safety instructions using the same structures, for example:
1 *Never…* (e.g. *Never smoke in the workshop. Never run along the aisles.*)
2 *No -ing* (e.g. *No smoking. No eating at work. No diving in the pool.*)

✱Tip
Top margin
Discuss this fact. It is surprising that such a big project came in almost 20% under budget. Compare this with recent projects such as the new Wembley Stadium, which is £400m over budget.

⚷ •●••	••●•	●•••
appropriate	automatic	designated
developing	exploration	generator
emergencies	horizontal	helicopter
kilometre	polystyrene	operator
	regulation	supermarket
	unfamiliar	

3 🎧 Get students to listen and check their answers, correcting them as necessary.

Pairwork

In pairs, first tell each student to work individually to match each text to the correct diagram. Check that they have done this correctly before they begin the pairwork. Then get each student to explain to the other how they think each type of foundation works.

Webquest

Students can work in small groups or pairs to do this research.

Key words

Go through the list of words to check students' pronunciation and understanding. Refer them to the *Glossary* if necessary.

➕ Additional activity

(stronger students)
Get small groups of students to work together to produce a short oral presentation on how skyscrapers are built. Each group can focus on one famous building they have researched in the *Webquest*, and use this as an example of the general process (which will be close to the information given in this unit). Each group member can be responsible for a different stage of the process. When they are ready, get the groups to come out and give their presentation.

10 Medical technology

Background

Medical technology applies engineering principles to the fields of biology and medicine, for example in the development of aids or replacements for defective or missing body parts. **Bioengineering** combines biological science with engineering.

One product of bioengineering is the artificial heart, which can extend and improve the lives of patients who might die of heart failure while waiting for a transplant of a natural heart. This device has been designed to have as few moving parts as possible and yet it has electric motors and a pumping system with hydraulic fluid and hydraulic valves. It has external and internal parts (that is, outside and inside the body). Inside the body is a rechargeable battery which powers the pumping system. This internal battery is recharged by an external battery using a simple electrical coil, which induces a current. This current then recharges the internal battery. The whole system is controlled by a microprocessor (also called a controller) inside the body. Of course, biological safety is very important, so the plastics used in the valves and hydraulic membranes of the artificial heart are durable enough to withstand 100,000 beats (or strokes) of the 'heart' per day, and designed not to damage blood cells or cause clotting. There is also a heart pacemaker, which is implanted under the skin and produces electrical pulses to cause the heart to beat at a regular and reliable pace or speed.

Another product of medical technology is **scanning** equipment. This scans internal organs, moving round the body at high speed creating images or pictures from a large number of different angles, using X-rays, ultrasound, and nuclear magnetic resonance. The CAT scanner uses special X-ray equipment. (CAT is really CT, which stands for Computed Tomography.) A computer processes the images to build up and display a cross section of the tissue and organs of the body. CT imaging is particularly useful because it can show several types of soft tissue with great clarity, helping radiologists to diagnose cancers and heart problems.

Electronic Assistive Technology or *EAT* (an example of **mechatronics**, which combines mechanical engineering, electronics, and IT) develops aids for severely disabled people. A house for someone with very limited movement, like the former Superman, Christopher Reeve, can be equipped with devices which permit him or her to control doors, lights, air-conditioners, televisions, computers, etc. with eye movements or by pneumatic switches, activated by sucking or blowing air.

Ultracane, as the name suggests, uses ultrasound (sound above the level of human hearing) to help blind people detect obstacles around them so that they can walk with more confidence. It has been nicknamed the 'batcane' as bats also use ultrasound to navigate. (Finding your location, as bats do, by echoes from sound waves is called echolocation.) The robot doctor in Gadget box is an experimental device on trial at St Mary's Hospital in London. Robot surgeons are also used for keyhole surgery. A robot's hand is slower than a surgeon's hand, but it has no vibration.

✱ Tip

induction of an electric current takes place when the current in one coil creates (or *induces*) an electric current in another nearby coil. The first coil does not touch the second.

Switch on

1 Get students to discuss the diagram and questions in pairs, without reading the text. Do not correct their answers until after the reading exercise in **2**.

> 1 Patients waiting for a transplant
> 2 A hydraulic pump and valve
> 3 The external battery powers the system. The internal battery has enough power to cover the time needed to change external batteries or to have a shower.
> 4 By induction
> 5 To decide the best heart rate at any time

2 Get students to read the text and check their answers. When they have finished, discuss their answers with the whole class.

Medical technology   43

* **Tip**
If students cannot remember *pneumatic*, remind them that the word was used in Unit 8 (*pneumatic sensor*). It is an adjective meaning *operated by air pressure* (see *Glossary*).

It's my job

1 Get students to discuss the questions in pairs before they listen. Do not correct their answers until after the listening exercise in **2**.

> 1 Electronic Assistive Technology
> 2 Moving their chin, blowing down a tube, or speaking
> 3 Mechanics, electronics, and software engineering
> 4 It turns the pages of a book.
> 5 By sucking or blowing down a tube

2 Ask students to listen and check their answers.

Language spot
Relative clauses

Refer to the *Grammar reference* on p. 120 for a full explanation of this language point. There is extra information about *non-defining* relative clauses but all the relative clauses in this *Language spot* are *defining relative clauses*, that is, they give essential information which serves to define the person or thing being described. They should not be preceded by a comma. Discuss the information and examples with the whole class.

1 Do this orally as a whole class exercise.

> 2 An X-ray technician is a person who specializes in taking and processing X-rays.
> 3 An X-ray camera is a device which takes pictures of bones and organs in the body.
> 4 A lab technician is a person who works in a scientific laboratory.
> 5 A kidney machine is a device which helps people with damaged kidneys.
> 6 A personal alarm is a device which people can use to call for help in an emergency.
> 7 A bioengineer is a person who applies engineering principles to medical problems.
> 8 A CAT scanner is a device which takes 3-D images of the brain and other organs.
> 9 A pacemaker is a device which helps people with heart problems.
> 10 A wheelchair is a device which helps people who cannot walk.

2 Get students to discuss these questions about the Ultracane in pairs. Do not check their answers.

3 Get students to write the answers individually.

> 1 who f   3 which c   5 which g   7 who a
> 2 which e   4 which b   6 who d

* **Tip**
ultrasound means sound waves which have a higher frequency than the human ear can hear.

➕ Additional activity
(weaker students)
In small groups, ask students to put a variety of objects on the desk in the centre of the group. You can also add some simple objects, such as a calculator, a protractor, a ruler, and so on. In turns, one student holds up an object and the next student has to make a short definition without naming it. For example, Student A holds up a calculator. Student B: *This is a device which calculates sums*. Write these words on the board: *device, tool,* or *instrument* and ask students to use them in their definitions.

44 Unit 10

⊕ Additional activity
(stronger students)
In small groups, students imagine they are designers of robotic devices for disabled groups. First ask each group to agree on one specific disability (such as deafness) and them tell them to brainstorm ideas for new robotic devices to help them. Later, get group leaders to report their ideas to the whole class.

Gadget box

Ask students whether they would like to be examined by the RP6 robot doctor. Get them to jot down some advantages and disadvantages for a few minutes, then discuss the topic with them. (Some advantages: *the patient has access to the most expert doctors even if they are far away; it stops doctors from wasting valuable time on travelling.* Some disadvantages: *patients may feel the doctor is not a real person; they may feel uneasy about being filmed; they may not talk freely to a camera.*)

Problem-solving

Get students to work individually at first, deciding on the best order. Then in small groups compare their answers and try to agree on a single best order. Encourage them to use the *Useful language* when they are expressing agreement, disagreement, and persuasion.

Vocabulary
Opposites

This exercise extends students' vocabulary study by practising another way to record and remember new words. Encourage students to note down opposites, where appropriate, when they record vocabulary.

a forwards	3 internal	e close / shut	g unwind
2 clockwise	d output	6 step-up gear	

Customer care
Giving clear instructions

1 In pairs, get students to read the instructions and decide whether they are clear and easy to follow, and if so, why. Discuss this with the whole class and elicit these points: the use of numbered steps, the use of titles for groups of steps (such as *Getting ready*), and the use of simple imperative verbs such as *take off, breathe, hold, count*.

2 Briefly discuss the battery-charging instructions with the class. Ask them how they could improve the instructions to make them easier to understand. Then get students to write a clearer set of instructions, using numbered steps.

⚬⊸ Possible answers
1 When you see two red lights flashing at the top of the joystick, this means it is time to charge the batteries.
2 Choose a well-ventilated place to charge the batteries.
3 Connect the charger supplied to the wheelchair and to the mains.
4 When the charger is connected, you will see a yellow light on the control panel.
5 Leave the charger connected until you see a green light. This means the batteries are fully charged.

3 Get students to exchange their instructions with one another to check the clarity and suggest improvements.

Medical technology **45**

*Tip
Top margin
Ask students to think of examples of new medical technology that might be considered 'miraculous', e.g. the pioneering face transplant performed in France.

Pronunciation
Linking words

1 🎧 Discuss and play the example. The linking of the final consonant of one word to the vowel sound of the next helps a speaker to sound more fluent and clear.

2 Get students to draw lines showing where a final consonant links with an initial vowel. Then ask them to read the compound nouns aloud.

> 🔑 1, 2, 3, 6, and 8 should be read with a clear link between final consonant and initial vowel

3 🎧 Get students to listen and repeat where necessary.

Writing
Short description

1 Set this as an individual writing task.

> 🔑
> 1 make images of internal parts of the body
> 2 printer
> 3 piezoelectric crystals
> 4 produce sound waves when current is applied across them
> 5 processes the data from the transducer to produce an image
> 6 an LCD monitor
> 7 stores the image along with patient details and other information
> 8 keyboard

2 Either individually or in small groups, get students to find out about CAT scanners. Tell students to write the description individually.

Pairwork

1 In pairs get students to discuss the topic and list their own ideas.

2 Get students to work individually, noting in the table what they think each device is for, and how it works. Then tell A and B to work together and describe their devices to each other.

3 Get each pair to decide on the six most important devices (out of the twelve) to ensure a safe environment for an elderly person living alone. If there is time, have a short class discussion, in which pairs of students explain their choices to the rest of the class.

Key words

Go through the list of words to check students' pronunciation and understanding. Refer them to the *Glossary* if necessary.

11 Personal entertainment

Background

The entertainment industry is one of the fastest growing areas of technology. Manufacturers have developed a range of personal entertainment devices designed for use by people on the move as well as larger home entertainment devices. All of this *hardware* depends on digital electronics.

Personal devices (which are often small enough to be handheld) include music players like Apple's iPod, portable media centres which can play video and audio, and portable games consoles such as Sony's Playstation Portable. **Home entertainment devices** include HD (high-definition) televisions, home games consoles which are plugged into a television and have controllers for a number of players to play against each other, and domestic cinemas which combine DVD players with hi-fi (high-fidelity) sound systems and flat panel LCD (Liquid crystal display) screens. Increasingly, devices combine a number of functions. Some mobile phones can play music, show videos, identify your exact position through the global positioning system, and provide wireless connections to the Internet.

Popular music is now commonly sold by downloading tracks (copying tracks to your hard disk) from Internet providers such as Napster. In the future it may be possible to download clips of films and TV programmes in the same way. A track is any short complete musical item such as a song or instrumental piece, a clip is a short piece of video or film. Illegal sharing of tracks damages the music industry because if everyone downloads tracks free of charge, the industry will make no money and eventually no-one will want to produce any music or films. To prevent this, the industry is taking a very hard line on anyone who is caught illegally downloading.

Video games have become big business. Companies such as Electronic Arts employ large teams to develop the software for new games. The teams include computer programmers (who produce the program code for the games), animators, and artists. There are many types of video games including racing games, FPS (First person shooters), RPG (Role-playing games), simulations (imitations of real-life situations) such as flight simulators or racing car simulators, adventure games, and sports games.

Some games are for individual use, others are team games, and some are for playing online with players around the world. MMOG (Massively multiplayer online gaming) is proving extremely popular because of the extra speed provided by **broadband** internet connections, and the possibility of receiving software **updates** (newer versions) quickly online. Some games have a more serious purpose. The US military uses video games and simulations in its training.

*Tip

portable hard disk devices include MP3 players, iPods, and similar portable devices which can download music from the Internet

MP3 stands for *MPEG Audio Layer 3*. It is a compressed digital sound file format. MP3 files are only around one-tenth the size of an original CD file, but the sound quality is the same. It is the most popular means of transferring music on the Internet.

Switch on

In small groups, ask students to find out how many in their group use each device for listening to music. Then get one or two members from each group to quickly collate the numbers, work out percentages for the whole class, and report the percentages to the class.

Listening

Opinions

1 Get students to listen and do the task individually. Tell them only to listen for the ways Max and Sam listen to music.

Max	Sam
live	CDs
online from Napster	albums
	MP3 player
	minidisks
	online

Personal entertainment **47**

2 🎧 Get students to listen and note down answers individually. Check their answers and then play the recording again, if necessary, to confirm their answers.

🔑 1 Napster
2 You can make your own music library and playlists. You can exchange tracks with friends.
3 Seven million
4 It's theft on a huge scale. It damages the music industry and cheats musicians.
5 People buy fewer CDs so the industry loses income.
6 Set up their own sites for selling online music. Go after anyone who downloads illegally.
7 CDs are over-priced. I don't see why we shouldn't share tracks with friends.

Language spot
should / shouldn't

Refer to the *Grammar reference* on p.120 for fuller information. Like other modals, the question form of *should* is a simple inversion: *I should …* becomes *Should I …?* The auxiliary *do / does* is not used with modals. The negative form simply adds *not*: *You should…* becomes *You should not / shouldn't…*.

Note this expression: *I don't think you should …*. This means the same as *I think you shouldn't…* but is much more commonly used.

1 Get students to do this individually.

🔑 1 You shouldn't download
2 You should
3 you shouldn't buy
4 you shouldn't share
5 you should buy
6 You shouldn't give
7 You should update
8 You shouldn't touch

2 Remind students that *should* and *shouldn't* are used when giving someone advice. Ask them what difference it would make if they used *must / mustn't* instead (this would change it from advice to an order or instruction).

🔑 1 You shouldn't be late.
2 You should dress smartly.
3 You should practise answering questions with a friend.
4 You should be honest. You shouldn't exaggerate your skills.
5 You should prepare some questions of your own.
6 You should read up as much as you can about the company.
7 You shouldn't look at the floor when you speak.
8 You should look at all the interviewers.
9 You shouldn't lean back and look bored.
10 You should sit straight and look confident.

➕ **Additional activity**
(weaker students)
Get each student to brainstorm a list of activities they would like to do one day, no matter how silly, difficult, or dangerous they might be (such as climb Everest, go bungee-jumping, dive to the Titanic wreck). Then, in small groups, tell each student to make statements such as *I'd like to dive to the Titanic one day. Should I do it?* Other students have to make positive or negative advice, depending on the student's skills, personality, etc: *Yes, you should. You're a good swimmer*, or *I don't think you should. It's too deep*.

It's my job

1 Before students read the text, ask them if anyone has an ambition to work in games design. Ask what qualifications and experience might be needed. Have a short discussion, and then set the task before they read the text.

Job	Work
Games Tester	plays games to find faults
Games Designer	creates ideas for games
Concept Artist	makes 2-D drawings of the characters
3-D Artist	makes 3-D drawings
3-D Animator	animates the characters
Producer	oversees and makes sure deadlines are kept and work goes to budget
Programmer	writes the program code required for the game
CGI expert	creates realistic slow motion action

2 Get students to read the text again and write the answers individually. Draw their attention to the meanings of *CGI* and *demo* in the Top margin.

1 You need experience to get a job and you can't get experience without one.
2 A degree in Computer science and a Master's (postgraduate) degree in Computer games technology.
3 He was part of a student team which won a prize for an idea for a video game. The prize allowed the team to develop the game.
4 Online gaming will expand. You'll be able to play games on many devices, not just consoles.
5 Medical and military simulations

Webquest

Students can work in small groups or pairs to do this research.

Vocabulary

New vocabulary

1 Get students to match the words with their definitions. Then discuss briefly what is meant by *a new use for old words*. Ask them for the old meaning of *burn, rip,* and *tag* (to *rip* an envelope open means to tear it open roughly; to *tag* something means to attach a tag, or label, to it). Ask them what two words are combined to form *podcast* (it combines *pod,* as in *iPod* and *broadcast*).

1 b   2 a   3 d   4 c

2 Students brainstorm a few words individually and write them down. Then get them to explain their meaning to their partners.

Problem-solving

1 Get students to do this individually or in pairs.

1 Strategy
2 Sports
3 A game where you are in charge of, for example, an army or a nation, and have to decide the best way to defeat the enemy or advance your country.

➕ Additional activity

(stronger students)
In groups, get students to simulate a meeting at work, where they have to analyze the reasons why certain genres sell well and others sell badly. Tell them that their company currently produces all the games listed in **2** in roughly equal numbers. Tell them the purpose of their meeting is to agree a change of sales strategy for their company. When they have finished their meeting, get one or two group members to present their decisions to the class.

Personal entertainment **49**

2 Get students to do this task in pairs.

2 Family and children's	6 Shooter
3 Action	7 Sports
4 Role-play	8 Adventure
5 Strategy	

✱Tip
Top margin
Ask students if they can think of any other names for afflictions caused by handheld electronic devices.

Customer care
Making suggestions

1 Get students to read the customer's email. Point out her use of the phrase *Dear Customer support* because she doesn't know the name of the support staff. The text of her email is very short and simple – she states the problem simply and asks for help.

2 Get students to read the reply. Point out that the writer gives a simple explanation, followed by a suggestion (*Try -ing*). Point out that the expression *That should work* is different in meaning from the use of *should* as advice. Here it means *I think (or hope) that it will work*. Mention the use of *Regards*, which is commonly used in emails, sometimes abbreviated to *Rgds*.

3 Get students to read the email and then compose a reply. Point out the friendly use of *Hi* and *Cheers* (which can mean *Thanks*).

✱Tip
Get students to practise saying email addresses out loud:
support at loudplay dot com
sam f at bluegrass dot com
lilly q at sojomail dot com
To clarify the spelling and spacing (which is very important in email addresses) the speaker may say
sam f – that's one word – at bluegrass – all one word – dot com
lilly q –one word – at sojomail – that's S-O-J-O-mail – all one word – dot com
Refer students to
Symbols and characters table on p.114.

Possible answers
To: lillyq@sojomail.com
From: support@loudplay.com
Dear Lilly
All our clips are in Windows Media format so check you have Windows Media Player installed. If you're sure you have it, check your system sound settings. Try turning up the sound. If that doesn't work, try turning up the sound on your media player.
Regards
Customer support

Pairwork

In pairs, get students to complete their table by asking each other questions. When they have finished, get them to check their answers by looking at each other's information.

Key words

Go through the list of words to check students' pronunciation and understanding. Refer them to the *Glossary* if necessary.

12 Information technology

Background

Information Technology (IT) is the application of **computers** to all aspects of technology. In this unit, the focus is on applications in car manufacturing. Computers are involved in every stage of car manufacture, including design, machining, assembly, ordering of parts, quality control, and distribution of the finished vehicle. To test vehicle safety, computers can simulate the effect of a crash test, which is much cheaper than crashing real vehicles. Computers can also simulate different assembly methods so that the best can be put into practice. They allow designs to be changed and defects (faults) corrected easily and quickly. They allow designs to be customized (manufactured following a customer's individual specifications).

CAD (Computer-aided design) has replaced working with paper and making **models** from wood, clay, or polystyrene (see Unit 3). CAD programs allow 3-D (three-dimensional) images to be produced on screen. Dimensions can be calculated easily and the forces acting on different parts of the structure can be shown. The data can be sent to a rapid modelling device which will produce a solid model.

Once the design has been approved, the complete CAD file is imported into a **CAM (Computer-aided manufacture)** program, where the machining operations are planned. This data is then converted into a set of instructions which can be read by a **CNC (Computer numerical control)** controller. This automates all the machine tools which manufacture the product. This whole computerized process from design to manufacture is known as **CADCAM**.

The term **CIM (Computer-integrated manufacturing)** includes CADCAM but takes the process even further. In CIM, all aspects of manufacturing including the supply of parts to quality assurance is computer controlled. This permits faster production times, a dramatic decrease in the number of workers required, and a lower risk of human error. CIM also allows manufacturers to move part of their operation to countries where costs are lower. For example, design may take place in one country and manufacturing in another. Where international collaboration involves different national companies in a single project, such as the Airbus, CIM enables parts to be designed and manufactured in different countries then transported to another location for final assembly.

In everyday personal computing, computers are attached to a range of peripherals (external devices). Some of these are input devices (which feed information into the computer, such as scanner, web camera, joypad, mouse, and so on. A wi-fi mouse communicates wirelessly with the computer). Output devices (which carry information out of the computer) include printers (laser, inkjet, or dot-matrix), and flatscreen monitors. Some peripherals are both input and output, such as voice-over internet protocol (VoIP) phones.

Switch on

1 Get students to work in pairs and brainstorm ideas.

2 Get students to do the matching exercise individually or in pairs.

O⊓ 7, 14, 8 a	3, 10 d	2, 16 g
6, 13, 5 b	4, 15 e	12, 8 h
1, 8, 5 c	9 f	11 i

3 Get students to work individually to make a list of uses for computers in their area of technology, then share their ideas with the rest of the class.

Information technology 51

✱ Tip
BrE spelling *program* is only used referring to a computer program (code) BrE spelling *programme* is used for other contexts, such as a study programme (course) or a TV or radio programme AmE uses the spelling *program* for all contexts

Reading
CADCAM

1 Get students to discuss this briefly with their partner. Then check the answers with the whole class.

> 2-D and 3-D CAD   CAM
> simulated crash   CIM

2 Ask each student, working individually, to note down what they think the terms mean. Then get them to scan the text quickly to find the answers.

> 1 Computer-aided design
> 2 Computer-aided manufacturing
> 3 Computer-numerical control
> 4 Computer-integrated manufacturing

3 Tell students to read the text more carefully and write a set of short notes, each one beginning with a verb as in the example. Then discuss answers with the class.

> calculate forces from a design   calculate when to replace tools
> simulate crash-testing   order new supplies
> simulate assembly   control robots
> control machine tools   inspect the finished vehicle
> control the assembly line   check paint thickness
> monitor supplies   check how well the doors fit

➕ Additional activity
(stronger students)
In small groups, ask students to consider this question: *How are computers involved in the sales, licensing, daily use, servicing, and scrapping of cars?* As a result of the discussion, they should produce a list of uses in note form, and then some members of the group should give a short explanation to the rest of the class, referring only to their notes. (Tell the groups not to write out the whole explanation.)

4 Get students to read the text again and do this task individually. Do the first one with the class as an example.

Past	Present
1 designs produced on paper	designs produced by CAD programs
2 dimensions calculated by measuring	dimensions calculated by CAD software
3 models made by hand	models made by rapid modelling devices
4 real cars crash-tested	simulated cars crash-tested
5 supplies ordered by staff	supplies ordered by computer
6 welding done by hand	welding done by robots
7 painting done by workers	painting done by robots
8 cars inspected by people	cars inspected by robots

✱Tip
Top margin
Discuss the quote. Ask students to find out how other Information Technology companies came up with their names, e.g. the name Google originated from a misspelling of googol which refers to 10^{100} (a 1 followed by one-hundred zeros).

Language spot
Past Passive

Refer to *Grammar reference* p.121 for more background information about the use of the Past Passive. Point out that the Passive is used because the speaker or writer wants to focus our attention on the process or action rather than who or what carries out the action.

1 Get students to do this exercise individually in writing based on the table in *Reading* **4**.

52 Unit 12

➕ **Additional activity**
(weaker students)
Get students in groups to brainstorm a list of simple activities which have changed over time. Tell them to write short notes about the past and present in two columns. (This will be similar to the one in *Reading* 4, but using everyday contexts.)
For example:

Past	Present
ride horses	drive cars
cook meals on fires	cook meals in ovens

Then they take turns to practise simple dialogues based on the table:
A *In the past, people rode horses.*
B *But now, they drive cars.*
Where appropriate, they should use the Past Passive:
A *In the old days, meals were cooked on fires.*
B *But now, they're cooked in ovens.*
Check the groups' lists for simplicity before they begin the dialogues.

🔑 1 Designs were produced on paper.
2 Dimensions were calculated by measuring.
3 Models were made by hand.
4 Real cars were crash-tested.
5 Supplies were ordered by staff.
6 Welding was done by hand.
7 Painting was done by workers.
8 Cars were inspected by people.

2 Get students to do this individually in writing. Tell them to add the second half to each sentence they wrote in the previous exercise.

🔑 2 Dimensions were calculated by measuring but now they are calculated by CAD software.
3 Models were made by hand but now they are made by rapid modelling devices.
4 Real cars were crash-tested but now simulated cars are crash-tested.
5 Supplies were ordered by staff but now they are ordered by computer.
6 Welding was done by hand but now it is done by robots.
7 Painting was done by workers but now it is done by robots.
8 Cars were inspected by people but now they are inspected by robots.

Listening

Describing changes

1 🎧 Ask students to read the information about Laura Santini, and get them to suggest any changes which they think have taken place in the food industry. Then get students to listen and note down the six changes mentioned.

🔑 1 Cans made from two pieces, not three
2 Faster process
3 Less metal used
4 Pull tabs on all our range
5 Labels printed onto the can
6 Half the workforce

2 🎧 When students have all completed their notes, get them to compare their answers with their partner, and make any necessary changes. Then play the recording again while they look at their notes.

It's my job

1 In pairs get students to discuss the questions. Do not correct their answers but get them to check their answers in the reading text.

2 Get students to write the answers to the questions. Check their answers.

🔑 1 Through an agency
2 You have to deal with people's emotions in addition to technical problems.
3 Frustrated and angry
4 You learn people-handling skills and quick thinking.
5 It's not well paid.
6 It's better paid, you deal with people face-to-face, and the work is more interesting.
7 Manufacturers' web sites and newsgroups
8 It's good for her future career.

Information technology 53

3 Do this orally with the whole class.

a soft skills   c trouble-shooting
b face-to-face   d taking calls

Customer care
Working on a help desk

1 Check that students understand the functions of the terms on the form. Next to *Advice given* they write a brief note explaining what advice they have given to the customer. If the problem is solved on the phone, they delete *No* next to *Cleared by phone*. If not, and a technician needs to visit the customer, they delete *No* next to *Requires visit*.

2 🎧 Get students to listen and complete the form. If they cannot complete it with a single listening, play the recording again.

Item	Printer
Location	Accounts
Make	HP
Model	LaserJet 2400
Problem	Not printing following a paper jam
Advice given	Check Status and Purge Print Document
Cleared by phone	Yes
Requires visit	No

3 Get students to role-play the help desk technician and the customer, using the form.

4 When they have finished 3, get them to read the *Listening script* on p.128 and note down any useful phrases.

*Tip
Top margin
Discuss the quote. Read them these other quotes about Information Technology that were also inaccurate.
'There is no reason for any individual to have a computer in his home.' Ken Olsen, President, Digital Equipment
'640k ought to be enough for anyone.' Bill Gates
'I think there is a world market for maybe five computers.' Thomas J. Watson, President, founder IBM

Vocabulary
Collocations

1 Get students to match A and B.

click on + an icon	scroll up / down + a page
calculate + costs	surf + the Web
display + information	select from + a menu
create + a new document	

2 Tell students to use words and phrases from 1.

1 information	4 costs	7 a new document
2 icon	5 the page	8 menu
3 pictures	6 the Web	

Pronunciation
-ed form of verbs and words with silent letters

Give a few examples when explaining about the three ways of pronouncing *-ed*. (For example *pushed* /t/; *closed* /d/; *moulded* /ɪd/.)

🎧 Get students to write the words into the correct columns as they listen.

🔑 /t/	/d/	/ɪd/
finished	controlled	constructed
mixed	customized	integrated
produced	damaged	invented
searched	disabled	operated
worked	planned	reflected

2 🎧 Get students to listen and check their answers. If they make many changes, let them listen once more to confirm their answers.

3 Let students discuss this for a short while with their partners and then take suggestions from the class. Try to elicit these rules from students (see *Tip*).

4 Get students to do this task individually. Check their answers.

🔑 1 lis~~t~~ening	4 ~~p~~neumatic	7 woul~~d~~
2 mi~~gh~~t	5 shoul~~d~~	
3 mode~~l~~ling	6 ve~~h~~icle	

5 🎧 Get students to listen and check their answers.

Speaking
Computer peripherals

Check students understand the meaning of *peripherals* by asking for examples *(printer, scanner, mouse, speakers)*.

1 When both students have completed the task, they can look at each other's page to check that they have identified the peripherals correctly.

2 Get students to work in pairs to do this task.

🔑 Input	Output	Input	Output
joypad	printer	VoIP phone (both)	VoIP phone (both)
Wi-Fi mouse	monitor	scanner	
web camera	speakers		

Webquest

Get students to complete the table individually and then to compare their answers and discuss any differences with others in the group.

In 2005, the five fastest computers were: Blue Gene, BGW, Columbia, Earth Simulator, Mare Nostrum. But the situation changes rapidly: for example, China is building a 100 teraflop computer and Japan has plans for a 10 petaflop (10 quadrillion) machine by 2011.

Key words

Go through the list of words to check students' pronunciation and understanding. Refer them to the *Glossary* if necessary.

✱ Tip
verbs ending in a /t/ or /d/ sound take /ɪd/
verbs ending in an unvoiced consonant such as /s/ take /t/
verbs ending in a voiced consonant or vowel take /d/

✱ Tip
Input – equipment that directs information into the computer, such as a mouse
Output – equipment that processes information coming out of the computer, such as a printer

✱ Tip
In measuring computer speeds the term *teraflop* means *trillion operations per second*.
kilo = thousand
mega = million
giga = billion
tera = trillion
peta = quadrillion

13 Telecommunications

Background

Telecommunications is a very important area of technology in a world where the fast transmission of larger and larger amounts of information (or **data**) is essential to the smooth running of business, government, and society. Globalization means that much of this information flow is international. The information transmitted can be sound, images, documents, data output from computers, and readings from measuring devices and instruments.

Telecommunications includes telephony, radio, television, email, fax, telemetry (measuring quantities at a distance), and data transmission from one computer to another in a **network**. Data is transmitted in the form of signals, which can take the form of electrical pulses (carried by copper cable or wire), light pulses (carried by fibre optic cable, made of glass or plastic), or radio waves (transmitted between antennas on the ground, or between satellite dishes on the ground and satellites in orbit around the earth). Fibre optic cables offer many advantages over copper cables. The capacity of copper wires to carry signals is limited. With fibre optic cables, many fibres can be bundled together allowing much more data (whether phone calls, TV channels, or internet data) to be carried. Radio transmissions have the advantage of covering wide areas, and not requiring the expense and trouble of laying and maintaining cables.

More and more information is now sent in digital format, while analogue systems are likely to disappear soon. Analogue systems use a continuously varying signal and are more likely to suffer from noise and interference. Digital systems use a stream of ON or OFF signals, which is more accurate and resists interference from external sources. Digital radio and high-definition digital television provide higher quality sound and pictures than analogue formats. The sounds and images we hear and see in real life are analogue, and therefore must be converted into digital format before they can be transmitted digitally. Older analogue devices such as telephones need an extra device, an analogue telephone adaptor (ATA) to adapt or convert analogue sound into digital signals, and analogue TV sets need a special adaptor box to convert digital TV signals into analogue pictures. Recent devices, such as IP phones and digital TV sets already have the adaptors built in.

Voice over Internet Protocol (VoIP) allows the Internet to be used for telephone communication. Data is compressed by the caller's computer and sent in tiny units (called packets), each travelling by different routes, decided by a device called a router. Each packet has its own unique identification and address, so the message can be reassembled by the receiving computer. VoIP offers much cheaper calls than traditional telephone systems.

Mobile phones (AmE cell phones) have become essential items for many people. They are, in effect, small radio transmitters: they convert sound into digital radio waves which are then transmitted via their antennas to the nearest mobile phone towers. New models are introduced every year with additional features. Text and photo messaging are usually standard. Most mobile phones allow Internet connections, include digital cameras, permit MP3 music files to be played, and have built-in navigation systems.

Switch on

1 In small groups, get students to brainstorm and choose one team member to write down all the possible ways of sending and receiving messages. Encourage them to think of unusual ways, such as *carrier pigeons, two cans joined by string, smoke signals, semaphore, Braille, sign language, tapping on a water pipe in a prison cell*, and so on. Get each group to report back to the whole class.

2 Get students to do this task individually.

A fibre optic cable
B satellite dish
C high definition television
D space satellite
E 3G phone
F digital radio

3 In pairs, get students to choose one device each and explain to their partner what it does. Note that this is a demanding task, and you will need to help weaker students with ideas and language. Give weaker students vocabulary prompts based on the key. (For example, 1 *orbit / receive / transmit / signal*).

> A Carries large amounts of data
> B Receives and transmits signals on earth
> C Receives digital television transmissions and displays a high quality TV picture
> D Orbits the earth. Receives and transmits signals
> E Receives and transmits telephone calls as well as live video and pictures
> F Receives digital radio transmissions

It's my job

1 Get students to listen and note down the answers to the questions.

> 1 Eight
> 2 Phone systems, satellite dishes, antennas, VHF radios, copper cables, fibre-optic networks, VoIP phones, a (telephone) line, a (satellite) dish.
> 3 Norway, Kenya, Belize
> 4 Voice over Internet Protocol

2 Get students to listen again and note down the answers to the questions. Discuss their answers, and play again where necessary.

> 1 In the army
> 2 Change from copper cables to fibre-optic cables. Change to VoIP phones
> 3 The equipment has got more complex and also lighter.
> 4 Being able to explain to clients quite complicated technology in simple terms
> 5 Working outside in bad weather

Language spot

Past Simple v Present Perfect

Discuss this question with the whole class. Elicit the answer that sentences 1–3 use the Past Simple because the speaker is talking about things that happened during his time in the army, a period of time that ended eight years ago. Sentences 4–6 use the Present Perfect because the speaker is referring to events which took place during a period of time up to the present. Sentence 4 refers to his time in the company, which is still continuing. Sentences 5 and 6 refer to his whole working life, which is also still continuing.

1 Get students to do this individually in writing. Discuss their answers.

> 1 has developed   6 has allowed   11 has meant
> 2 invented   7 have been   12 have (now) developed
> 3 was   8 started   13 has made
> 4 started   9 began
> 5 made / have made   10 has allowed

2 Get students to do this individually. Discuss their answers.

Telecommunications 57

1 have you been	5 joined
2 trained	6 Have you seen
3 were you	7 we've replaced
4 served	8 we've introduced

Gadget box

Discuss the DoCoMo network. Ask students how long it will be until this technology will be available in their countries. The fingerprint scanner is a protection from fraud and only the registered user can use the electronic wallet.

Pronunciation
Past Simple v Present Perfect

Quickly revise the difference in form between the Present Perfect and Past Simple. Before playing the recording, discuss the first item and elicit that 1a is the Present Perfect and 1b is the Past Simple. If students are in any doubt, discuss a few more examples in this way before playing the text.

🎧 Then get students to listen and tick the sentence they hear in each pair.

1 a   2 a   3 b   4 b   5 a

➕ Additional activity
(weaker students)
In pairs or small groups, students ask each other questions beginning *Have you ever ... ?* Students reply truthfully: *No, I haven't* or *Yes, I have*. If they answer *Yes, I have*, the questioner asks a follow-up question: *When did you ... ?* to which the answer is *I did it* + time expression. For example: **A** *Have you ever dived from a boat?* **B** *Yes, I have.* **A** *When did you do that?* **B** *I dived from a fishing boat two years ago.*

Speaking
Mobile phones

Get A and B to ask each other questions and complete the table. When they have both completed the task, let them look at each other's information to check their answers.

Reading
VoIP phone systems

1 In pairs, get students to discuss the questions before looking at the text.

1. Voice over Internet Protocol
2. Bits of compressed digital data sent via the Internet
3. A place near which you can make and receive calls with a VoIP headset

2 Get students to do this individually.

2 b   3 f   4 a   5 g   6 d   7 c

✱ Tip
Top margin
Discuss the quotes. Ask students to research other firsts, such as radio and TV programmes

➕ Additional activity
(stronger students)
In pairs, get students to role-play a VoIP salesperson explaining to a customer how VoIP works using the information in *Reading* 1 and 2, but without looking at the Student's Book. Get the customer to act as if he / she knows very little about it, and to keep asking questions to clarify points.

Customer care
Explaining in simple terms

1 Set this exercise before the lesson, and ask each student to search for information on the device or process they have been given. Then in the lesson, get them to explain it to each other in pairs.

✱ Tip
BrE spelling is *analogue*
AmE spelling is *analog*
The two recommended websites are American and so the American spelling of *analog* is given in the exercise.

2 🎧 Play the recording twice, and ask students to make notes, as follows: first, make notes about content; second, note down useful words and phrases. Ask students to read out their notes, and give them some feedback on what they have noticed.

Webquest
Satellite communications systems

1 Get students to study the diagrams and answer the questions. Get weaker students to do this task in small groups. Check that weaker students know the meaning of *orbit*.

> 1 24 hours
> 2 Three
> 3 It is easier to launch them into their orbiting position around the Equator.
> 4 TV, radio, telephony, broadband services, military communications, video-conferencing, etc.

*Tip
Geostationary orbit moves at the same speed as the Earth's rotation, so that it appears to be stationary at the same location above the Earth. *Coverage* means the area of the Earth's surface which can receive a signal from the satellite. *Global coverage* means that the whole of the Earth's surface receives the signal. Ask students for examples of other words with the prefix *geo-*, meaning the Earth (*geology, geography, geometry*).

2 Get students to read the text and the table. Check that they understand the difference between *geostationary* (see *Tip*) and *geosynchronous* (explained in the Student's Book).

3 Get students to choose one of the systems mentioned and complete the form in the same way. Stronger students can do all three systems. Weaker students can work in small groups, checking different web sites and sharing the information.

System	SES Astra
Used for	Digital TV and radio
Number of satellites	Twelve
Altitude	36,000 km
Orbit	geostationary
Coverage	global
System	Eutelsat
Used for	TV and radio, broadband, business TV, video-conferencing
Number of satellites	24
Altitude	–
Orbit	geosynchronous
Coverage	Europe, Middle East, Africa, India, parts of Asia and the Americas
System	Worldspace
Used for	radio, telephony
Number of satellites	Two
Altitude	41,200 km
Orbit	geosynchronous
Coverage	Africa, most of Asia and Europe

Key words

Go through the list of words to check students' pronunciation and understanding. Refer them to the *Glossary* if necessary.

14 Careers in technology

Background

The jobs described in this unit are types of engineers and technicians. The difference between an engineer and a technician (see Unit 2) relates to qualifications and responsibilities. Engineers should have a better understanding of the principles and theories behind their discipline, and are more likely to be involved in design and project management, or running an industrial complex. Technicians require a practical understanding of their specialism, and have the practical skills and understanding of equipment to convert the engineers' theoretical design ideas into working solutions.

Most engineers will work as a member of a team including engineers from other disciplines. This is why employers try to recruit people who are good team players and have good communication skills, in addition to their engineering skills and qualifications. Each engineer will have technicians working for them to make parts or assemblies, conduct tests, and perform other tasks as part of the team. Here are some examples of engineering and technician jobs:

- **Environmental Engineers** who work in a manufacturing industry will know what conditions (or environment) a product will have to survive and operate in, for example the extremes of temperature and humidity that it will be exposed to. They must also be able to devise tests that will ensure that the product will be safe for use. They must make sure that the product and its parts can be recycled or safely disposed of after they are no longer in use. The term Environmental Engineer can also refer to an engineer who works directly in environmental protection, using technology to prevent or reduce pollution and other dangers to the life or health of humans, plants, and animals.
- **Petroleum Engineers** specialize in the exploration and production activities of oil companies. They have to implement high technology plans in often very dangerous conditions, ranging from Arctic to desert temperatures, and from land to the deep ocean.
- **Sound Technicians** have a working knowledge of many disciplines including electrical engineering, electronics, and sound recording equipment studios.
- **Aerospace Engineers** apply engineering principles to spacecraft, aircraft, satellites, and rockets. Their work involves the control of flight, aerodynamics, jet engines, etc.
- **Agricultural Engineers** design agricultural machinery and equipment. They are concerned with ways to improve the processing of agricultural products and with conserving soil and water.
- **Biomedical Engineers** apply engineering principles to the development of **prosthetic** (artificial) devices, to replace or support damaged organs or limbs. They also develop diagnostic and treatment devices such as scanners.
- **Chemical Engineers** apply chemistry (combined with maths and economics) to the process of converting materials or chemicals to more useful or valuable forms, for example, converting natural gas into a range of plastics.

Switch on

1 Ask students to work individually for a few minutes, choosing jobs from the list.

2 In small groups, get students to tell each other which jobs they have chosen, and the reasons for their choice.

*Tip

job title – the title (or description) of the person doing the job, for example *Civil Engineer*.
areas covered – all the technical subjects or fields which the person will work in, for example *construction*, *transport*, and *power requirements* – the qualifications, skills, and experience which an applicant must have, such as *diploma* or *good teamworker*

Reading
Job descriptions

In groups of three, get each student to choose a different job description, read it, and make notes about the job using the four points given. When they have finished making their notes, tell them to take turns to describe their job to the group. Check that they are reading from their own notes, and not directly from the texts.

Unit 14

Language spot
Job requirements

Refer back to the texts from *Reading*. Ask students if they know the difference between *essential* and *desirable* requirements for a job. (*Essential* – applicants who do not have them will not get the job. *Desirable* – applicants who have them are more likely to get the job.) Explain that *must* is used for *essential* or *necessary* requirements, and *should* is used for *desirable* or *preferred* requirements. Point out the negative form: *You mustn't be colour-blind = It's a requirement not to be colour-blind*.

1 Get students to do this exercise individually in writing.

> 1 You must have a diploma in engineering.
> You must be a good team player.
> You should have good communication skills.
> You should be physically fit.
> You mustn't be afraid of heights.
> You mustn't be colour-blind.
> 2 You must have a certificate or diploma in engineering.
> You must have good mathematical and computing skills.
> You should be willing to travel.
> You should be able to explain complex requirements in clear terms.
> 3 You must have a diploma or degree in petroleum engineering.
> You must be willing to travel.
> You must be willing to spend long periods in difficult environments.
> You should be a good communicator.
> You should be able to supervise others.

2 Get students to write notes under two headings: *Essential requirements* and *Desirable requirements*.

> Essential: Prepared to work irregular hours and to travel
> Desirable: Certificate or Diploma in electrical engineering, electronics, or audio-visual communication or other technical areas
> Practical skills in carpentry and construction
> Theatre experience

3 Ask students to do research about the job requirements of a career they are interested in. (The *connexions* site gives careers information to young people and students in the UK.)

Writing
CV

1 Discuss the CV with students.

2 Get students to complete their own CV with real information about themselves.

✱ Tip
Top margin
Discuss the salaries. Ask students if they would like to earn this amount of money, and also to consider the life of an Offshore Petroleum Engineer.

✱ Tip
Things to do when hunting for a job:
- scan *job advertisements* in newspapers, magazines, and the Internet
- complete a *CV*
- write a *letter of application*
- obtain the agreement of one or more *referees*

If you are *short listed* (selected as a suitable candidate), you can expect to be interviewed by a *panel*, so prepare for the *interview*.

✱ Tip
CV (curriculum vitae) – a full description of your working life, including previous work experience, qualifications, and skills
referee – a person (such as a former employer or tutor) who can recommend you as a potentially good employee, and write a *reference* for you

➕ Additional activity
(weaker students)
In groups, students brainstorm a list of well-known jobs and sporting and other activities, such as footballer, Olympic swimmer, airline pilot, parachutist. In turns, one member of the group says one of the activities, and other members make statements about job requirements.
Example: Student A: *a pilot*. Student B: *He must have good eyesight*. Student C: *She should like travelling*. Student D: *He mustn't be afraid of heights*.

Careers in technology **61**

*Tip

European CV format – a proposed standard for use within the European Union
competences (countable noun) – specific skills or behaviours which are necessary to qualify someone to do a job
competence (uncountable noun) – general ability to do a job well

*Tip

Top margin
Discuss the mistakes in the note at the top of p.101. Ask students if they know any other words that often fool the spellchecker.

*Tip

Top margin
Discuss the rules. Explain that the more you prepare for an interview the more you will impress your interviewers.

Pairwork

1 Check that students know the meanings of words such as *ambitious, orderly,* etc. in the questionnaire.

2 In pairs, get students to ask each other questions from the questionnaire, and then choose the best adjective from the list (*realistic,* etc.) to describe their partner.

3 Get students to choose a good job or career for their partner. Their partner can disagree!

4 Now students have to think about themselves. Get students to choose the terms (from the list) which best describe their own qualities.

5 Get students to write a short personal statement about themselves, using the example as a model. When they have finished, pairs read their statements to each other and try to improve their statements together.

Pronunciation
Stress in long words (2)

1 🎧 a 3   c 2   e 5   g 3   i 5   k 3
      b 5   d 3   f 4   h 4   j 7   l 2

2

1 ●●●	2 ●●●●	3 ●●●●
capacity	anticlockwise	animator
dependable	energetic	enterprising
development	entertainment	indicator
environment	information	motivated
peripheral	simulation	ventilated

Speaking
Job interview

1 Get students to work in pairs, A (interviewers) and B (job applicants). Put the As in one group, and the Bs in another group. Tell the As to prepare suitable questions for the applicant and anticipate questions from the candidate. At the same time tell the Bs to list the questions they may be asked and to prepare answers. When they are ready, in pairs, As and Bs, role-play the interview.

2 🎧 Play the interview and then get the pairs to switch roles. Role-play the interview with A as the applicant and B as the interviewer.

Key words

Go through the list of words to check students' pronunciation and understanding. Refer them to the *Glossary* if necessary.

➕ Additional activity

(stronger students)
In groups, students prepare a set of guidelines (in note form) for being a successful interviewee. They should include both essential points (such as *never be late for the interview*) and desirable points (such as *wear clothing that is smart but not too formal*). When their notes are ready, ask the groups to present their recommendations to the class.

15 The future of technology

Background

Large companies such as British Telecom employ their own futurologists to predict the most likely developments so that investment can be targeted on these areas. However, it is very hard to predict future developments in technology with any certainty, especially beyond a horizon of five to ten years. One way to do this is to look at current technological developments, and imagine how things will be if they continue into the future. Here are some possibilities:

It is likely that intelligent machines such as **robots** will be used much more than they are at present. One possible area is surgery where computer-controlled robot arms can, in some cases, operate with more precision and less chance of error than a human surgeon. Intelligent machines can also be used in telemedicine to help doctors diagnose and treat patients at a distance, even in different countries.

Nanotechnology (technology involving tiny particles) is already being used to create miniature machines small enough to be injected into the body to deliver drugs to the correct place or to destroy dangerous cells. This will probably be developed much more in the future.

In transport, features such as satellite navigation already exist now in a small number of cars, and may become standard in all cars. Satellites will probably be used to provide instant and accurate information on road congestion, which will be useful for drivers to be able to choose the quickest route to their destination. This technology will also allow precise and automatic congestion charging, so drivers can be charged for using the busiest roads. In order to do this, devices will have to be installed in all cars. In the distant future, road vehicles may come under computer control on main roads to ensure safe speeds are maintained and there is no danger of collision with other vehicles.

In all branches of technology computers will play a greater role and these computers will be faster and more powerful than today's. This will allow and encourage new devices to be invented, in the same way as much of today's innovative technology (such as CADCAM car manufacture and wireless telecommunications) were made possible by increased computer power and speed.

Unfortunately, not all new applications will benefit society. Computer crime, such as identity theft and credit card fraud will continue. As more of our personal information is stored electronically we will become more vulnerable to hackers. Applications designed to make warfare more efficient will continue to be funded by governments around the world.

Switch on

In small groups, get students to discuss the predictions and note down either specific dates or decades (e.g. *the 2030s*.) Discuss the difficulty of really predicting the future.

✻ Tip

If you do not have the facilities to divide your class and have them listen to different recordings, treat the *Listening* exercise as a normal listening exercise. In **3** have a general class discussion about what was said in the recording.

Listening

Predictions

Briefly discuss what a *futurologist* does. Ask students if they think it's a real job.

1 🎧 Get students to work in small groups, A and B. Get all the A groups to listen only to Lianne's comments and all the B groups to listen only to Stefan's comments. Get them to tick the boxes as they listen.

Lianne (Group A)	Stefan (Group B)	Prediction about
	✓	transport
✓		health
✓	✓	IT
✓		telecommunications
✓		military
	✓	crime
✓		domestic
✓	✓	developing countries

2 🎧 Get the same groups to listen to the same speaker again (A to Lianne; B to Stefan) and make short notes about the predictions.

3 Tell each student from the A groups to work in pairs with a student from the B groups. Get them to explain their speaker's predictions to each other, and then decide which predictions they accept. Tell them to make a short list of the predictions. When they have all finished, briefly get some of the pairs to report their decisions to the whole class.

Language spot
Phrasal verbs

Get students to brainstorm some common phrasal verbs, such as *pick up, switch on, take off*, etc., and write them on the board, pointing out the structure *verb + adverb* or *preposition*. Discuss the example of the two meanings of *look up*. Refer to the *Grammar reference* on p.123 for more information on phrasal verbs. Draw students' attention to the word order and the examples: a noun object can take two positions, but a pronoun object can only appear between the verb and the adverb.

1 Before students do the exercise individually, do one or two examples with the whole class.

1 carry out	5 work out	9 plug in, switch on
2 give up	6 shut off	10 print out
3 find out	7 set up	11 switch off
4 cut down	8 close down	

➕ Additional activity
(weaker students)
In groups, students design and write an advertisement for Wakamaru the robot. The advert should list all the household jobs the robot can do, using some of the ideas from the brainstorming in *Gadget box*.

Gadget box

Discuss the robot with the class, and then hold a brief brainstorming session in which students suggest other tasks they would like a robot to perform. Then ask them what tasks they would *not* like it to perform, and why.

Pronunciation
Linking in phrasal verbs

Explain that phrasal verbs can be difficult to understand because (a) the words are short and can be spoken quickly, and (b) the final consonant of one word often links with the initial vowel of the second so that you can't always tell where one word ends and the other begins.

* Tip

An extra problem with short phrases such as *cut them off* or *line them up* is that short pronouns like *them* or *him* are often shortened to *'em* and *'im*: some people may say *cut 'em off*, which can sound like one word *cutemoff*.

1 🎧 Play the examples before students look at the book and ask students what they think the individual words are.

2 🎧 Get students to listen and draw lines to mark the linking. Check their work, and then play the words again.

1	Line them up.	5	Find it out.	9	Plug it in.
2	Give it up.	6	Shut it down.	10	Turn it on.
3	Work it out.	7	Start it up.		
4	Switch it off.	8	Print them out.		

3 After they have tried this once, remind them of the linking exercise in **2**, and then see if they can improve their speed the second time round.

4 Choose the funniest tongue-twisters, and ask pairs to demonstrate their creative ability and speed in front of the class.

Pairwork

Get students to make notes of the main points in their text. Then, put them in pairs, A and B. Get them to explain the main points to their partner. Tell them to listen carefully and take notes based on what their partner has told them. Finally, tell the pairs to work together and compare their notes with the texts.

* Tip

Top margin

Draw students' attention to the quote at the top of p.107, made in 1890, about the telephone. Ask them what this tells us about prediction.

➕ Additional activity

(stronger students)

In small groups students think of (a) more examples of words using the affixes given; and / or (b) more affixes commonly used in English for technology, with some examples of words and their meanings.

* Tip

Some additional affixes commonly used in technical words:
geo (the Earth)
sol (the Sun)
therm (heat)
mono (one)
multi (many)

Vocabulary

Affixes

1 Explain what is meant by *affix*. Ask students why they think it is useful to learn the meanings of common affixes used in technical words (it will help them work out the meaning of an unknown word). Tell them to look at the table and study the affixes and their meanings.

2 Get students to do this exercise individually. Explain that they have to find a word for each meaning. At first, some students may think that this is a very difficult exercise. Tell them that in fact it is very simple if you use affixes. Do one or two examples: *tele* (an affix from the table meaning *at a distance*) + *medicine* (given in the exercise) = *telemedicine*.

1	telemedicine	5	prestressed concrete	9	cordless phone
2	microchip	6	supercomputer	10	biometrics
3	polycarbonate	7	microprocessor		
4	micrometer	8	extractor fan		

Customer care

Saying goodbye

Treat this exercise as a fun way of finishing the book. Discuss the way that some people use *See you later* or *Later* even when they do not expect to see you later.

Quiz

Put students into groups of three. Students organize the quiz as explained in the Student's Book.

A (Units 1–5)
1. pollution, easy communications
2. faster, more efficiently
3. length, wingspan, weight, capacity
4. Antilock Braking System
5. eer
6. See the list on p.10.
7. I like calculus. Simple Present used to describe thinking and feeling.
8. *generating and supplying power* (or similar).
9. electronics
10. Design software used by civil engineers and others.
11. See the list on p.17.
12. prototype
13. Any of the names on p.21 or any other well-known designer.
14. The product requirements.
15. *Why do you use plastic?* (or any other substance which can be moulded).
16. Steel, aluminium alloy, titanium, carbon fibre.
17. Elasticity
18. Strength
19. Sports clothing
20. A material built up from layers.
21. wind, wind up, unwind
22. engage
23. combustion, compression
24. ten to the power minus twelve
25. oscillating

B (Units 6–10)
1. See p.34.
2. Handcuffs
3. Personal Identification Number
4. An air-tight seal
5. Recognize its owner's grip.
6. Aluminium alloy
7. *by, using, by using*
8. injection moulding
9. Kevlar
10. *which uses, powered by*
11. Advanced Safety Vehicles
12. a hybrid
13. heavy batteries, limited range, need to recharge batteries
14. congestion
15. apologizing
16. cladding
17. *fireproofed*
18. burn
19. Eye protection must be worn.
20. mat
21. To allow the patient to charge the external battery or unplug it to have a shower.
22. a pneumatic switch
23. *which helps people with heart problems.*
24. ultrasound
25. backwards

C (Units 11–15)
1. Computer-generated Imaging
2. demonstration
3. burn
4. *shouldn't, mustn't*
5. a games tester
6. Computer Integrated Manufacturing
7. simulate
8. *were*
9. /t/
10. *p*
11. See the pictures on p.92. Other answers are possible.
12. *I've been*
13. *packet switching*
14. Liquid Crystal Display
15. 1971
16. Civil Engineer
17. See the job description on p. 99.
18. *mustn't*
19. CV (Curriculum vitae)
20. employer
21. *prediction*
22. *up*
23. *give*
24. an intranet
25. very small

Key words

Go through the list of words to check students' pronunciation and understanding. Refer them to the Glossary if necessary.

Instructions for communication activities

General instructions for information gap activities (1, 2, 6, 9, 11)

1. Divide students into pairs.
2. Give Student A worksheet to one student of each pair, and Student B worksheet to the other. Ask them not to look at each other's worksheet.
3. Student A asks questions and obtains information from Student B and completes his / her worksheet.
4. The students switch roles, with Student B asking Student A questions and completing his / her worksheet.
5. When they have both completed the task, the two students look at each other's worksheet and check their answers.

General instructions for group presentation activities (5, 15)

1. Divide the class into groups of 3–6 students and give all the members of each group the same information. For example, Group A members receive the same Group A material.
2. The groups discuss the material and prepare their presentations. Encourage them to add their own information and ideas, and if there is time they should prepare a large visual. Each member of the group should be responsible for a different part of the presentation.
3. If the groups need help, sit with them and discuss the topic.
4. When they are ready, get each group to give its presentation in front of the class.
5. Give feedback on the clarity of each group's explanation.

Unit 1

1. Follow the general instructions for information gap activities.
2. When students have completed the information gap activity, they work individually and write sentences under the *Comparison* column comparing the two computers.

> **Possible answers**
> The Pacer is shorter than the Joshiba.
> The Joshiba is wider than the Pacer.
> The Joshiba is thicker than the Pacer.
> The Joshiba is heavier than the Pacer.
> The screen of the Joshiba is larger than the (screen of the) Pacer.
> The Joshiba has a bigger memory than the Pacer.
> The Pacer has a bigger hard disk than the Joshiba.
> The Joshiba is more expensive than the Pacer.

Unit 2

1. Follow the general instructions for information gap activities.
2. In this activity, divide students into groups of three. A is a second year part-time engineering student, B is a first year part-time engineering student, and C is the engineering college secretary. C should be the strongest student in the group.
3. While the pairs of students are talking, go around the groups and encourage them, whenever appropriate, to use the Present Simple when talking about the normal timetable and the Present Continuous when talking about the temporary timetable.

> Student A: **Mon** Theory / Practical, **Tue** Maths / Laboratory, **Wed** English / Project
> Student B: **Mon** Lab / Maths, **Tue** English / Self-study, **Wed** Project / Practical

Unit 3

1. Divide students into pairs.
2. Give Student A worksheet to one student of each pair and Student B worksheet to the other.
3. Before the quiz, students work individually, filling the gaps in the questions. Check their work (see key below). Weaker students might need help. This would be a good opportunity to go through how to form questions.
4. When they are ready, Student A quizzes Student B and takes a note of the score.
5. Student B quizzes Student A and takes a note of the score.
6. They compare scores. Then the teacher finds out which student(s) in the class had the top scores.

> **Student A:** 1 is   2 is   3 called   4 produced
> 5 did   6 invented   7 do   8 made
> **Student B:** 1 does   2 called   3 produced
> 4 do   5 did   6 does   7 invented
> 8 made

Unit 4

For Tasks 1–3, divide students into small groups and get each group to appoint a chairperson and a reporter (who will take notes). Task 4 is an individual writing exercise based on the decisions made by the student's group in Task 3.

Task 1 Tell students to use materials and properties they have learned about in this unit. One student should act as reporter and make notes of the materials and properties. The groups will need to refer back to the notes when they are holding their meeting.

> **Possible answers**
> a helmet – polycarbonate – hard, impact-resistant
> b pack – polyester – weather-resistant, tough
> c gloves – nylon – durable, weather-resistant
> d rope – nylon – elastic, strong in tension (= when it is pulled)
> e sunglasses – polycarbonate – lightweight, tough, hard
> f jacket – polyester – lightweight, breathable
> g trousers – Kevlar – stretchable, wear-resistant
> h boot soles – plastic – moisture-resistant, good grip

Task 2 Explain that this is part of a meeting between two engineers who work in a company designing sports equipment. The engineers, Peter and Louise, have to decide which materials to use for some new climbing equipment. There are two mistakes in the memo.

> In Decision 1, Change the word *light* to *tough*. In Decision 2, change *a mixture of nylon and Kevlar* to *Kevlar*.

Task 3 Each group has a meeting similar to the one in Task 2, but covering two or more different items of equipment / clothing from Task 1. The reporter takes notes of the decisions and the reasons.

Task 4 This task is optional and could be done for homework. Students write memos individually using the notes of the decisions taken in their group's meeting. Tell them to use the memo in Task 2 as a model.

Unit 5

1. Follow the general instructions for group presentation activities. In this activity, all groups are working on the same information.
2. If the groups need help, sit with them and discuss the topic. Use this background information:

   Name of system: Solar water heating system.
   Purpose of system: To provide a supply of hot water for taking showers in a building using solar energy, without the need for an electrical or gas heater.
   Main components and what they do:
   solar water heater panel – heats the water
   water tank – collects and stores the water
   hot and cold valve – turns on hot and cold water and mixes them
   shower head – heated water comes out through this
   connecting water pipes – carry water between the components
   cold water inlet – brings cold water into the system

   How the system works: Cold water enters the system through the cold water inlet. It flows through the pipes via the water tank and into the solar water heater panel. The sun heats the water as it passes through the panel. The heated water flows from the panel through the valve and out through the showerhead. When the valve is closed, hot water flows into the top of the water tank. In the tank, hot water stays at the top, and cold water sinks to the bottom. When the valve opens, pressure from the cold water inlet pushes warm water out of the top of the tank.

Unit 6

1. Follow the general instructions for information gap activities.
2. Explain the scenario, as given in the worksheet. One of the students is a salesperson and the other is a customer. The customer has to phone the salesperson and explain his / her security problems. The salesperson has to listen, ask questions, and finally recommend the best device. The customer then writes the key information in the table, in note form.

Unit 7

1. Divide the class into pairs.
2. Students read the information then prepare their presentations. Give them help converting the active verbs into passive.
3. Students give their presentations to their partners.

68 Instructions for communication activities

Unit 8

1. Divide the class into groups of three.
2. Make one photocopy per group and cut it into sections. Give the top section (the task and table of advantages and disadvantages) to the whole group.
3. Give each student a different set of information. If a group has fewer than three students, give stronger students two sets of information.
4. Before the groups begin work, check that they all understand the meaning of terms in the tables such as *power*, *efficiency*, and *range*. The headings *smoke* and *carbons* refer to smoke pollution and emission of greenhouse gases, respectively.
5. Without showing their information to the others, students in each group discuss the advantages and disadvantages of each form of fuel and then complete the chart. One student in the group is appointed to write the group's ideas in the table.
6. Students should then have a conversation about the implications of using these fuels in the future based on exercise 3 in the *Grammar test*, if this has already been used. They should use the correct modal verbs.

Unit 9

1. Follow the general instructions for information gap activities. However, there is no change of roles at the end of this activity.
2. Explain the situation, as given in the worksheet. Student A is a safety inspector, conducting a survey of safety procedures at Three Valleys Construction site. Student B is the site manager of the Three Valleys Construction site. Student B should be the faster reader of the pair.

> 🔑
> A 8 – findings examples 1 (2 accidents), 2,
>   3 (2 accidents), 4, 6, 7.
> B 7 – findings examples 1 (2 injuries), 2, 3, 4, 6, 7.
> C 0
> D 18 – findings examples 1 (8 breaches), 2, 3 (2 breaches), 4, 5 (3 breaches), 6, 7, 8.
> E 2, 8, 1, 3, 1, 1, 1, 1

Unit 10

Before you start, go through the pictures to revise the vocabulary. Ask students what the pictures represent and what the people / devices do. Encourage relative clauses: *It's a hearing aid, a device which helps people with hearing problems.* Explain to the students that this is a memory game.

1. Divide the class into groups of 3–5.
2. Give each group a sheet, cut up into cards.
3. Each group shuffles the cards and then places them upside down in 7 x 4 formation.
4. The group play *The Memory Game*:
   - The first player turns up two cards.
   - If it is a match (i.e. picture matches text) he / she takes both cards away and keeps them. He / she then turns up another two cards, again keeping them if they are the same, but …
   - If they are different, he / she turns the two cards face down in their original position.
   - The turn passes to the next student, who turns up two cards.
   - As the game progresses, the players will have seen more cards and should try to remember where certain words and pictures are placed and so should be able to locate the card that matches the one they have turned up.
   - In order to make the game more communicative, encourage the students to discuss the devices they have found, using relative clauses as much as possible.

Unit 11

1. Follow the general instructions for information gap activities.
2. There should be a total of four calls as each student has two problems. Once the first problem has been solved the student will encounter a second problem that will require a second call to the hotline technician.

Unit 12

1. Divide the class into groups. This is a group collaborative activity.
2. Each group studies the keys (with examples) and then solves the coded messages by deciding which key to use.

> 🔑
> 1. computer-aided design – key: 1234567 ➲ 4325761
> 2. computer-aided manufacturing – key: 123456789 ➲ 583972146
> 3. computer numerical controlled – key: move alphabet three places back A ➲ D, B ➲ E etc.
> 4. computer-integrated manufacturing – key: move alphabet two places back A ➲ C, B ➲ D etc.

3. Each group invents a code and sets a puzzle for other groups to solve. Time the groups, and announce the fastest one.
4. If the second two parts of the activity seem too difficult for your group, ask them to use the codes in the activity to send each other messages.

Unit 13

1. As pre-activity homework, tell students to find out what they can about the advantages and disadvantages of using VoIP rather than normal landline telephones.
2. Divide the class into small groups.
3. Give half the groups the Group A information (advantages of VoIP). Give the other groups the Group B information (disadvantages of VoIP).
4. Tell the groups to prepare their side of the argument in a class discussion. Tell them to discuss the information given and to add any more points they have discovered from their own research.
5. Tell the groups also to try to guess what the other side's points will be and to discuss how to counter their arguments.
6. When the groups are ready, divide the class with all the A groups on one side and all the B groups on the other. Tell students they are acting the part of senior staff in a company trying to decide whether to change from landlines to VoIP in the company. At the end of the discussion, they will vote whether or not to make the change.
7. Chair the discussion, and then hold the vote.

Unit 14

1. Before this lesson, make sure that each student has completed his / her own personal CV (word-processed if possible) as explained in the Student's Book, p.101. Tell students to bring four copies so all group members have one.
2. Divide students into groups of three or four, and choose one student in each group to be the interviewee. Tell the interviewee to give copies of his/her CV to the other students in the group. Check that each group member has the CV of the person being interviewed.
3. Give each group the top half of the sheet. The group, including the interviewee, works together to complete the job advertisement giving details of a job which they would like to apply for. Make sure they use details that are compatible with the CV of the interviewee.
4. Divide each group into sub-group A (the interviewing panel, working together) and sub-group B (the interviewee, working alone) and give out Student A and Student B worksheets.
5. Tell the interviewing panel (A) to prepare questions to ask the interviewee, based on his / her CV and the job advert. Tell them not to show their questions to the interviewee before the role-play.
6. Tell the interviewee (B) to prepare ideas and replies to expected questions from the panel, based on his / her CV and the job advert. Tell him / her not to show these to the panel before the role-play.
7. When students are ready, get the groups to role-play their interviews. These can be done simultaneously, or if there is time, groups can perform in front of the class. Give feedback on the interviews.

Unit 15

1. Follow the general instructions for group presentation activities.
2. Divide the three different ideas among the teams. If possible, give these out before the lesson, and ask the groups to do some research on these ideas.
3. At the end of each presentation, the class questions the team, asks about any disadvantages of their ideas, and votes to give funding to the team with the most impressive future technology.

1 Grammar test

1 Complete the table with adjectives from the list. Put one simple adjective next to the correct rule. Then write its comparative form. There are two adjectives for each gap.

bad	combustible	fast	portable
big	early	large	safe
cheap	far	noisy	slim

Rule	Simple	Comparative
Add -er	quiet _____1	quieter _____2
Add -r	wide _____3	wider _____4
Double final letter and add -er	thin _____5	thinner _____6

Rule	Simple	Comparative
Change final -y to -i and add -er	heavy _____7	heavier _____8
Change the word (irregular)	good _____9	better _____10
Use *more*	expensive _____11	more expensive _____12

2 Use the information in the table to complete the sentences comparing the two cars.

	Saloon	Sports
Size	6 passengers	2 passengers
1 Year of manufacture	2002	2004
2 Maximum speed	150 kph	180 kph
3 Acceleration to 80 kph	15 seconds	10 seconds
4 Fuel capacity	70 litres	40 litres
5 Price	€ 40,000	€ 25,000

EXAMPLE The saloon car is designed for a family, so it is much *larger than the sports car*.

1 The sports car is about two years _____.
2 When you drive at the maximum speed, the sports car is _____.
3 The saloon car accelerates to 80 kph _____.
4 The sports car has a _____ fuel capacity _____.
5 The saloon car is _____.

3 Choose the correct words to complete the sentences.

1 This _____ is broken, so please call a _____ to repair it.
   mechanic / mechanical / mechanism
2 A _____ is someone who has been trained in _____.
   technical / technology / technician
3 After the _____ installation, the building will have _____.
   electricity / electrical / electrician
4 Study _____ at university if you want to become an _____.
   engine / engineer / engineering
5 He has a diploma in _____ and now he repairs _____ equipment.
   electron / electronics / electronic

1 Communication

Student A
Ask questions to find out the specifications of Student B's laptop computer. Write the specifications in your table. Then check your answers by looking at Student B's diagram. Finally, write sentences comparing the two laptops.

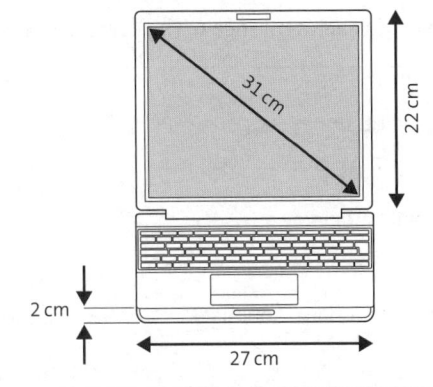

	Pacer XJ100	Joshiba 850T	Comparison
length	27 cm		The Pacer is shorter than the Joshiba.
width	22 cm		
thickness	2 cm		
weight	1.1 kg		
screen size	31 cm		The screen of the …
memory	64 MB		The _____ has a bigger memory …
hard disk	3.0 GB		
price	£450		

Student B
Ask questions to find out the specifications of Student A's laptop computer. Write the specifications in your table. Then check your answers by looking at Student A's diagram. Finally, write sentences comparing the two laptops.

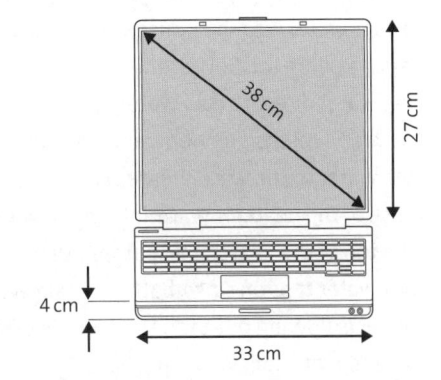

	Pacer XJ100	Joshiba 850T	Comparison
length		33 cm	The Joshiba is longer than the Pacer.
width		27 cm	
thickness		4 cm	
weight		1.5 kg	
screen size		38 cm	The screen of the …
memory		256 MB	The _____ has a bigger memory …
hard disk		2.5 GB	
price		£925	

2 Grammar test

1 Join each sentence to the correct rule, and then to the correct tense.

1. Ice melts above freezing point.
2. Lessons start at 9 a.m. every day.
3. The polar ice caps are rapidly melting.
4. The weather feels very cold today.
5. When you press the button, the alarm sounds.
6. The fire alarm is ringing.
7. What do you like about your course this year?
8. I have four weeks' holiday every year.
9. The oil flows into the tanker via this pipe.
10. World population is steadily increasing.
11. How often do you go to the gym?
12. This exercise now seems very clear to me.

A always true
B happening now
C routine action
D thinking and feeling

Present Continuous
Present Simple

2 Read the description of a process and underline each verb. Then rewrite the verbs that are in the incorrect tense.

This is how the water system <u>operates</u> in a house. First, a pipe brings water into the house. A stop valve just inside the building ~~is controlling~~ the flow of this water. From here, pipes are carrying the water direct to cold water taps on sinks and baths, and to valves on toilets, showers, and washing machines. Pipes also take the water to the water heater. Here a heating element near the base of the heater is warming up the water. The hot water rises to the top of the heater, and passes out into the hot water pipes to hot water taps on sinks, baths, and showers. Finally, the dirty water is flowing out of the sinks, toilet, shower, and bath through a system of wider waste pipes.

_____
_____
controls
_____
_____
_____
_____
_____
_____
_____
_____

3 Complete the interview using the Present Simple or Present Continuous form of the verbs in brackets.

I _____ ¹ (be) a student and I _____ ² (study) Electronic Engineering. Normally, we _____ ³ (attend) lectures and _____ ⁴ (carry out) experiments in the laboratory. But this week we _____ ⁵ (do) real work with Electronic Engineers in various different companies. I _____ ⁶ (work) in a company called TeleNorth, which _____ ⁷ (install) radio-based local area networks. I _____ ⁸ (help) an engineer, Fred Johnson, to assess where to put the transmitters. Today, we _____ ⁹ (visit) a company that _____ ¹⁰ (build) a new factory and wants to use TeleNorth technology for its networks.

2 Communication

Student A
You are a second year part-time engineering student. You see this notice in your college department:

> **TIMETABLE CHANGED THIS WEEK DUE TO TWO-DAY HOLIDAY.**
>
> **PLEASE PHONE ENGINEERING DEPARTMENT SECRETARY (x 1245) FOR TEMPORARY CHANGES TO TIMETABLES.**

Phone the department secretary to find out the changes to your timetable this week. Correct your timetable.

Weekly timetable

	09.00–10.30	11.00–12.30
Mon	Theory ✓ (NO CHANGE)	Practical _____
Tue	~~Practical~~ MATHS	Theory _____
Wed	Self-study _____	Maths _____
Thur	~~Laboratory~~ HOLIDAY	~~Laboratory~~ HOLIDAY
Fri	~~English~~ HOLIDAY	~~Project~~ HOLIDAY

> Useful language: do Maths   study English   go to the lab   do Self-study   work on my project   have Theory

---

Student B
You are a first year part-time engineering student. You see this notice in your college department:

> **TIMETABLE CHANGED THIS WEEK DUE TO TWO-DAY HOLIDAY.**
>
> **PLEASE PHONE ENGINEERING DEPARTMENT SECRETARY (x 1245) FOR TEMPORARY CHANGES TO TIMETABLES.**

Phone the department secretary to find out the changes to your timetable this week. Correct your timetable.

Weekly timetable

	09.00–10.30	11.00–12.30
Mon	Laboratory ✓ (NO CHANGE)	~~Laboratory~~ MATHS
Tue	Theory _____	Practical _____
Wed	Theory _____	Practical _____
Thur	~~Project~~ HOLIDAY	~~English~~ HOLIDAY
Fri	~~Maths~~ HOLIDAY	~~Self-Study~~ HOLIDAY

> Useful language: do Maths   study English   go to the lab   do Self-study   work on my project   have Theory

---

Student C
You are the secretary of the college engineering department. First year and second year (Y1 and Y2) students phone you to find out about changes to this week's timetable. Ask students which subjects they normally study and tell them the changes to their timetable.

Changes to timetables of all students for this week only

		09.00–10.30	11.00–12.30
Mon	Y1	Laboratory ➔ NO CHANGE	Laboratory ➔ Maths
	Y2	Theory ➔ NO CHANGE	Practical ➔ NO CHANGE
Tue	Y1	Theory ➔ English	Practical ➔ Self-study
	Y2	Practical ➔ Maths	Theory ➔ Laboratory
Wed	Y1	Theory ➔ Project	Practical ➔ NO CHANGE
	Y2	Self-study ➔ English	Maths ➔ Project
Thur	Y1	Project ➔ CANCELLED (HOLIDAY)	English ➔ CANCELLED (HOLIDAY)
	Y2	Lab ➔ CANCELLED (HOLIDAY)	Lab ➔ CANCELLED (HOLIDAY)
Fri	Y1	Maths ➔ CANCELLED (HOLIDAY)	Study ➔ CANCELLED (HOLIDAY)
	Y2	English ➔ CANCELLED (HOLIDAY)	Project ➔ CANCELLED (HOLIDAY)

3 Grammar test

1 Look at the picture and read the specifications. Then complete the table by writing questions for the answers.

Prompt	Question	Answer
Colour?	*What colour are the headphones?*	They are black and silver.
1 Weight?		They weigh 195g.
2 Weight includes cables?		Yes
3 Headband adjustable?		Yes
4 Width ear cushion?		It's 7.6 cm wide.
5 Includes extension cord?		Yes
6 Length cord?		It's 1.5m long.
7 Batteries or electricity?		They use both.
8 Number batteries?		1 battery
9 How carry?		In the case
10 Cost?		They cost £150.

Specifications of headphones

Colour: silver and black
Headphone: 19.5 cm H x 16.5 cm W
Ear cushion: 9.65 cm H x 7.6 cm W
Weight with cables: 195g
Headband adjustable to 7.5 cm
Box contains:
- 1 pair of headphones
- 1.5m extension cord
- Stereo phone adapter
- Dual plug adapter
- 1 AAA battery
- Carrying case

Price: £150

2 Find the information you need and complete the questions about the gadget.

The wall-mounted CD player was designed by Japanese designer Naoto Fukasawa[1] just for fun[2] in 1999[3]. Now it is one of the top-selling products at Muji.

Dimensions: 17[4] x 17 x 4[5] cm
- Colour: white[6]
- Price: £79.00
- Buy from? Muji Co UK[7]
- Buy online? Yes[8]
- Shipping: £4.95[9]
- Total price: £83.95[10]
- Delivery: within five days

1 *Who designed the CD player?*
2 Why _____ ?
3 When _____ ?
4 How wide _____ ?
5 How thick _____ ?
6 What _____ ?
7 Which company _____ ?
8 Can _____ ?
9 How much _____ ?
10 What _____ ?

3 Communication

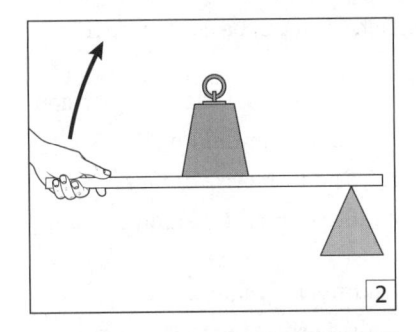

Technology quiz
Student A
Complete the questions with the correct form of the verbs in brackets. Then ask Student B the questions and check his / her answers.

1 How tall _____ the world's tallest building? (be)
   a > 500m   b < 500 but > 450m   c < 450m
2 What kind of lever _____ this? (be)
   a first class   b second class   c third class
3 What's this _____? (call)
   a bar code   b PIN   c zip code
4 Who _____ the first chemical battery in 1800? (produce)
   a André-Marie Ampère   b Alessandro Volta   c James Watt
5 Which of these _____ Leonardo da Vinci (1452 – 1519) not design? (do)
   a helicopter   b speedboat   c submarine
6 Who _____ the World Wide Web? (invent)
   a Bill Gates   b President Clinton   c Tim Berners-Lee
7 What _____ the letters *RA* stand for in *RADAR*? (do)
   a **RA**dio   b **R**eflected **A**lternate   c **R**ed **A**lert
8 Who _____ the first yo-yo? (make)
   a ancient Japanese   b ancient Koreans   c ancient Romans

Answers: 1a, 2b, 3a, 4b, 5b, 6c, 7a, 8c

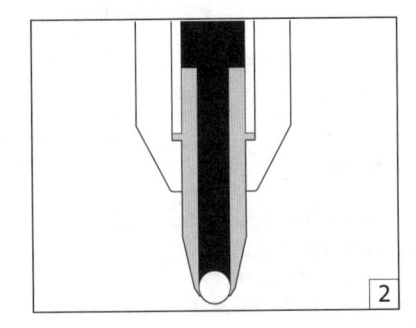

Technology quiz
Student B
Complete the questions with the correct form of the verbs in brackets. Then ask Student A the questions and check his / her answers.

1 Which gas _____ a light bulb contain? (do)
   a oxygen   b nitrogen   c argon
2 What's this device _____? (call)
   a printer head   b ballpoint pen   c inkjet
3 Who _____ the first internal combustion engine in 1885? (produce)
   a Henry Ford   b Kiichiro Toyoda   c Gottlieb Daimler
4 What _____ the letters *LA* stand for in *LASER*? (do)
   a **L**os **A**ngeles   b **L**ight **A**mplification   c **LA**mp
5 When _____ the World Wide Web start? (do)
   a 1990   b 1985   c 1995
6 What _____ an MP3 player do? (do)
   a transports people   b plays music   c plays games
7 Who _____ the mercury thermometer? (invent)
   a Anders Celsius   b Gabriel Fahrenheit   c Baron Kelvin
8 Who _____ the first scissors? (make)
   a ancient Egyptians   b ancient Greeks   c ancient Chinese

Answers: 1c, 2b, 3c, 4b, 5a, 6b, 7b, 8a

4 Grammar test

1 Complete the sentences with *of, from, for,* or *to*. Each word can be used more than once.
1 Aluminium is lightweight and has excellent resistance _____ corrosion.
2 This is why a lot of plane parts are made _____ aluminium.
3 Carbon-fibre is used _____ making professional bicycle frames.
4 Polyurethane is used _____ make footballs because it is highly resistant _____ impact.
5 Cro-moly is an alloy. It is made _____ a number of metals.
6 Kevlar or nylon is used _____ manufacturing climbing ropes.

2 Make sentences from the table. Use the direction of the arrows to help you.

EXAMPLE   *Polycarbonate is used for making sunglasses.*
          Footballs are made of polyurethane.

polycarbonate	⮕	sunglasses
footballs	⬅	polyurethane
1 composites	⬅	plastic & many fibres
2 fibreglass	⮕	hulls of sailing boats
3 sails of sailing boats	⬅	polyester
4 bike helmets	⬅	polycarbonate & polystyrene

3 Complete the table about the properties of different materials.

This plastic *has* good resistance to water.	This plastic *is* very water-resistant.	This plastic *resists* water well.
Kevlar has excellent elasticity.	Kevlar _____ ¹ very elastic.	Kevlar stretches and _____ ² (return) to its own shape.
Titanium has very good resistance _____ ³ corrosion.	Titanium _____ ⁴ highly corrosion-_____ ⁵.	Titanium _____ ⁶ corrosion very well.
Polyurethane _____ ⁷ excellent flexibility	Polyurethane _____ ⁸ very _____ ⁹.	Polyurethane _____ ¹⁰ (bend) very easily.

4 Make pairs of sentences using the words in the table

EXAMPLE   *Polyurethane has excellent elasticity and weather-resistance. This is why it is used for making footballs.*

Material	Properties	Uses
polyurethane	excellent elasticity, weather-resistance	footballs
1 fibreglass	tough, slightly flexible	arrows
2 polystyrene	good heat-resistance, lightness	bike helmets (insides)
3 polycarbonate	transparent, high scratch-resistance	sunglasses
4 titanium	hard, corrosion-resistance	ship propellers

4 Communication

1 In your group, discuss the answers to these questions.

What materials do you think the different parts of the climber's equipment are made of?

What properties do you think the materials have? Why are they useful?

2 Read this extract from a meeting and correct the mistakes in the memo below.

Peter	What material do you think we should use for the new helmet?
Louise	I think polycarbonate would be best.
Peter	Why?
Louise	Well, it's tough and it resists impact.
Peter	Yes, you're right. OK, what about the new rope? Should we use nylon for that?
Louise	No, I don't nylon is appropriate. I think we should use Kevlar.
Peter	Why?
Louise	Well, it's wear-resistant. It's also fatigue-resistant.
Peter	OK, I agree. Let's use Kevlar.

Memo
To: General Manager
From: Design Engineer
Date: 20 May 20—
Subject: Materials for new sports products

As you know, Louise and I held a meeting to discuss materials for our new sports equipment. We decided the following:

1 We should use polycarbonate to make the new helmet. This is because the material is light and impact-resistant.
2 We should use a mixture of nylon and Kevlar for making the new rope. This is because it won't wear away and will resist fatigue.

If you would like to discuss these ideas, please let me know.

---

3 Have a meeting using your group's ideas about the best materials for climbing equipment.

4 Write a memo to your manager explaining the decisions your group made in the meeting.

5 Grammar test

1 Match pairs of actions.

a press the alarm button
b turn the steering wheel clockwise
c click on the 'save' button
d turn the steering wheel anticlockwise
e the pendulum of the clock oscillates
f push down the camera button
g the piston moves in a reciprocating motion
h rotate the volume knob clockwise

1 then, the camera takes a picture
2 at the same time, the sound on the radio becomes louder
3 at the same time, it turns the camshaft in a rotary movement
4 at the same time, the car moves to the left
5 then, the program stores your data on the hard disk
6 at the same time, the spring becomes tighter
7 then, a loud bell rings
8 at the same time, the car turns to the right

2 Join the pairs of actions from **1** and make sentences using *when* or *as*.

EXAMPLE
a + 7 *When you press the alarm button, a loud bell rings.*
b + 8 *As you turn the steering wheel clockwise, the car turns to the right.*

3 Complete the sentences with *before* and *after*.

1 You must put on your helmet _____ you can enter the building site.
2 You can only enter the site _____ you put on your helmet.
3 You must wash your hands _____ you handle chemicals.
4 You can only come into the factory _____ you show ID at the entrance.
5 They must be trained to operate the machine _____ they can use it.
6 He can only become an engineer _____ he completes his degree.

4 Look at the diagram of a brake system. Join each pair of sentences using *when* or *as*.

EXAMPLE
The foot presses the brake pedal. Immediately after this, the piston moves down the master cylinder.
When the foot presses the brake pedal, the piston moves down the master cylinder.

1 The piston moves down the cylinder. At the same time, the oil in the pipe transmits pressure to the brake pad.
2 The pressure of the oil pushes the pad against the disc. Immediately after this, the wheel slows down and stops.
3 You release the brake pedal. Immediately after this the piston moves up the cylinder towards the pedal.
4 The piston returns up the cylinder. At the same time, it removes pressure from the oil in the pipe.
5 The pads move away from the disc. Immediately after this, the wheel is able to move freely.

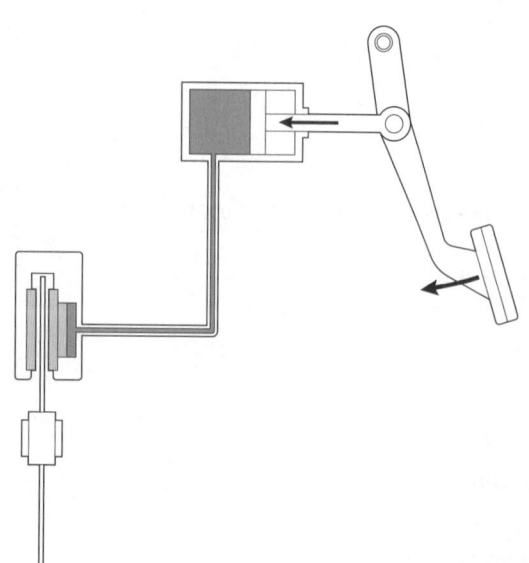

5 Communication

Your group is a team of designers and engineers who specialize in appropriate technology for rural villages in developing countries. Your team has designed this system for low-cost solar water heating. Discuss the system with your group and make notes in the table. Then, with your group, give a brief presentation to the class of how the system works.

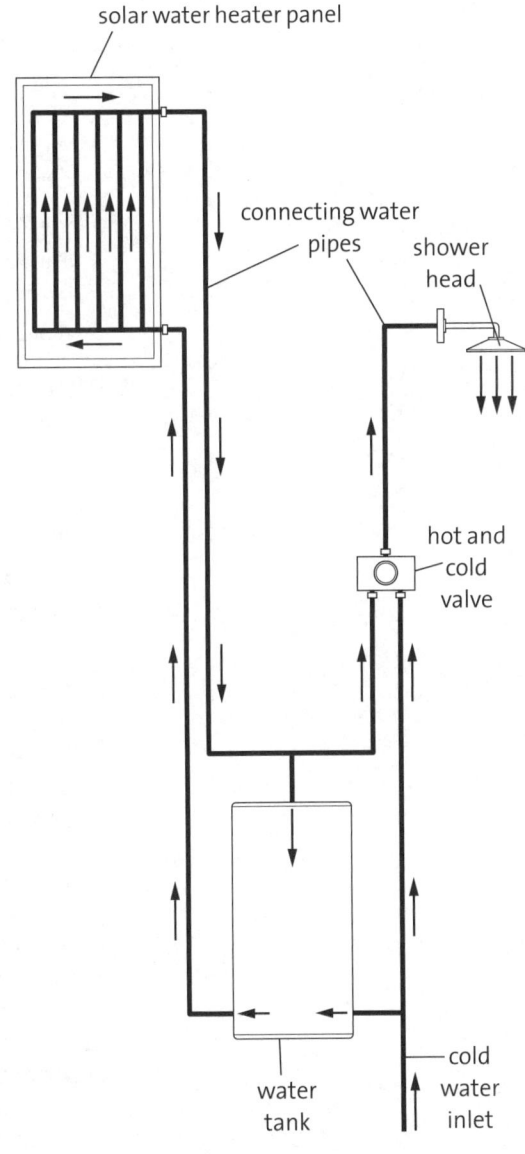

Name of system: Solar water heating system

Purpose of system: _____

Main components:	What the main components do:
1 _____	_____
2 _____	_____
3 _____	_____
4 _____	_____
5 _____	_____
6 _____	_____

How the system works: _____

6 Grammar test

1 Rewrite each sentence using the Present Simple form of the verb in *italics*.

   EXAMPLE   The X-ray device at an airport is used for *detecting* dangerous items inside luggage.
   The X-ray device at an airport detects dangerous items inside luggage.

   1 The purpose of the GPS navigation system is to *locate* your position anywhere on earth. *(Begin: The GPS navigation system…)*
   2 The Rotundus spherical robot is used for *patrolling* and *guarding* buildings and sites.
   3 The Flashcam is used to *warn* people not to commit a crime.
   4 The function of dynamic grip recognition is to *allow* a gun to be used only by its owner.
   5 A police officer's job is to *protect* the public and to *catch* criminals.

2 Complete the sentences using the words in brackets, making any necessary changes to their form.

   1 Anti-viral software is used for _____ (protect) computers.
   2 The sensors in the Rotundus are used to _____ (detect) movement, smoke, heat, and sound.
   3 A police officer's Kevlar jacket acts as a _____ (protect) against bullets.
   4 The purpose of a taser is _____ (incapacitate) a suspect without injury.
   5 An X-ray machine is used for _____ (monitor) passengers' luggage.
   6 Smoke alarms are used to _____ (warn) people about fires.

3 Complete the text with *as*, *for*, or *to*. Each word can be used more than once.

   On any passenger aeroplane there are several safety devices and items of equipment which are used _____ [1] protecting the passengers and _____ [2] prevent accidents or death during an emergency. For example, every seat has a seat belt. This is used _____ [3] holding the passengers secure during sudden and violent movement of the plane. There are several doors which can be used _____ [4] emergency exits if necessary. Every plane carries first aid kits. The purpose of this equipment is _____ [5] allow cabin crew to treat any injury safely. Above every seat is an oxygen mask, which acts _____ [6] a ventilator if the air pressure in the cabin suddenly drops. Another important safety item is the life jacket under every seat. This is designed _____ [7] prevent drowning. When the life jacket is filled with air, it floats in water and acts _____ [8] a support for the passenger in the water.

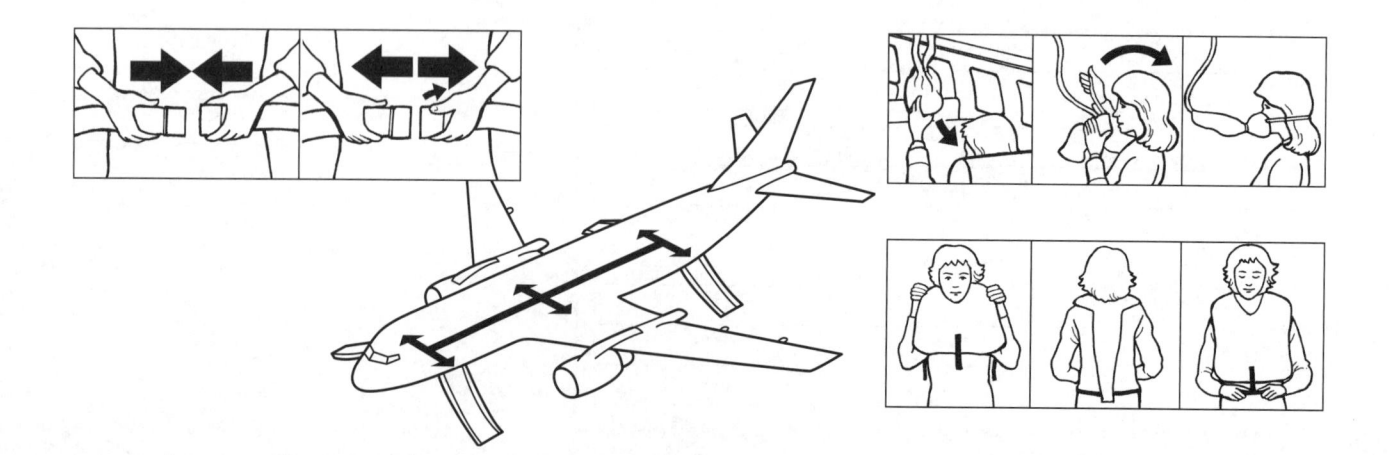

6 Communication

Student A

1 You are a salesperson working in a company which manufactures security devices. A customer phones you for advice. Ask the customer questions about his/her problems, then recommend the best device. Use the sales catalogue to help you.

Sales catalogue

Security device	Detects	Typical applications
Heat-sensitive fire alarm	heat	Prevents fires before they start.
Optical intruder alarm	motion	Senses an intruder in the building.
GPS locator	location	Locates company vans and lorries by satellite.

2 You are the new head of security for a government building. You have a series of possible security problems, so you phone up a company that manufactures security devices. Explain your problems to the salesperson, ask for recommendations, and complete your notes.

Problem	Device to detect	Best device
Terrorists and criminals use weapons made of plastic. Normal X-rays cannot detect them.		
Criminals can steal tasers and use them against security staff.		
Intruders can enter our offices because they can steal entry passwords, or even steal ID cards.		

Student B

1 You are the director of security for a company that stores goods in warehouses and delivers them by lorry. You have some security problems, so you phone up a company that manufactures security devices. Explain your problems to the salesperson, ask for recommendations, and complete your notes.

Problem	Device to detect	Best device
Intruders break into warehouses. Then they move around undetected, stay a long time, and steal goods.		
Machinery catches fire easily if it overheats. We need a device to detect heat before a fire starts.		
We need to trace stolen company lorries. We also need to keep track of our staff – they sometimes use vans for their own business.		

2 You are a salesperson working in a company which manufactures security devices. A customer phones you for advice. Ask the customer questions about his/her problems, then recommend the best device. Use the sales catalogue to help you.

Sales catalogue

Security device	Detects	Typical applications
Dynamic grip taser	unique hand grip	Prevents unauthorized people from holding it.
Super X-ray bag check	plastic	Detects plastic weapons and explosives.
Fingerprint ID card	fingerprints	Prevents criminals from using stolen ID cards or passwords.

7 Grammar test

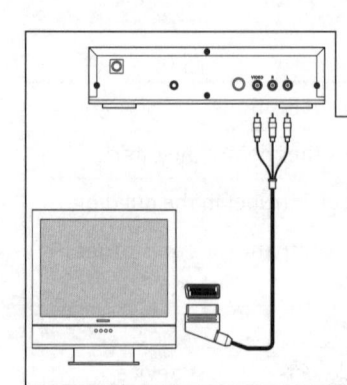

1 Write a description of the process from the notes. Use the Passive form of the verbs in *italics* and *First, Then, Next, Now*.

EXAMPLE   *First, the plug is pushed into the socket. Then, the scart...*

Quick-start guide to your new TV *and* DVD player

push plug into power socket
insert two AAA batteries into remote control
set TV channel to 'AV'
place disc onto door
connect scart cable between TV and DVD player
switch on power
press OPEN/CLOSE button on DVD player to open door
touch OPEN/CLOSE button again to close door

2 Write sentences from the information in the table using the Present Passive form of the verbs.

(Note: only include the agent with *by* if you think the information is important.)

EXAMPLES   *Car components are assembled by robotic machines in modern factories.*
Metal is shaped using a range of processes.

Agent	Verb	Object	Where / When / How / Why
robotic machines	assemble	car components	in modern factories
people	shape	metal	using a range of processes
1 welders	bond	steel plates	using different types of welding
2 suction devices	remove	loaves	from their tins
3 they	mould	plastic parts	using extrusion or other processes
4 huge saw blades	slice	loaves	in a high-speed slicing machine
5 you	fill	the hopper	first
6 they	remove	plastic parts	from the mould when they are cold

3 Change the dialogues into sentences.

EXAMPLE   **A** How is plastic loaded into the moulding machine?
B They use a hopper.
Plastic is loaded into the moulding machine using a hopper.

1 **A** How is the plastic melted?   **B** They use heaters.
2 **A** How is the melted plastic pushed along the barrel?   **B** They use a ram.
3 **A** How is dough made to rise?   **B** They use yeast.
4 **A** How are the loaves taken out of their tins?   **B** They use suction.
5 **A** How are the loaves sliced?   **B** They use giant saw blades.

4 Complete the text with *to*, *by*, *in*, or *from*. Each word can be used more than once.

How is steel made? It's made _____¹ removing most of the impurities _____² iron. Why must the impurities be removed? They have to be removed _____³ make the metal stronger and less brittle. The iron is changed into steel _____⁴ an oxygen furnace. Here, the iron is heated to a very high temperature _____⁵ remove the impurities. The high temperature is achieved _____⁶ blowing oxygen into the molten iron.

7 Communication

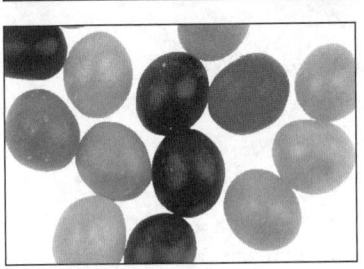

Student A

You work for a sweet-making factory. Your new job is to give tours of your factory to visitors. Before taking the visitors on tour, you give them a short presentation about the manufacturing process for your top-selling product: the *Exploding Bombshells*. Last week you interviewed and recorded the Production Manager about the manufacturing process. This is what he said:

Step 1 We make the *Exploding Bombshells* in large rotating pans. We heat the pans with gas flames. We add sugar to the pan, and we make a sweet from each grain of sugar.

Step 2 The sweet-maker, or *panner*, adds liquid sugar to the pan. The liquid sugar sticks to the sugar and makes a hard shell. The *panner* repeats this process 100 times.

Step 3 The *panner* adds colour and flavour.

Step 4 We put the sweets into a polishing pan to give them a final glaze.

Step 5 We package the *Exploding Bombshells* in a bagging machine. We measure the amount of sweets and we place the correct amount in each bag.

Step 6 We heat seal the bags to keep in freshness.

Step 7 A conveyor belt carries the bags to the display containers and shipping boxes.

Now prepare and give a presentation to your partner as practice before you face the visitors. Remember that you should use the Passive when giving a presentation about a manufacturing process.

Start your presentation like this:

The Exploding Bombshells are made in large rotating pans.

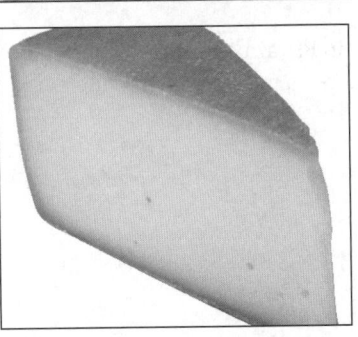

Student B

You work for a cheese-making factory. Your new job is to give tours of your factory to visitors. Before taking the visitors on tour, you give them a short presentation about the manufacturing process for your cheeses. Last week you interviewed and recorded the Production Manager about the manufacturing process. This is what she said:

Step 1 We collect the milk from local cows, and we inspect and weigh it.

Step 2 Then we transfer the milk into stainless steel silos and we heat it.

Step 3 We then pump the milk into enclosed cooking vats and we add bacteria.

Step 4 After that the milk forms a mass which we cut into loaf shapes with knives.

Step 5 We drain the loaves of water by pressing them.

Step 6 Through the whole process we minimize the handling of the cheese by using semi-automatic machine operations.

Step 7 Finally, we package the cheese in the high-speed computer-controlled packager.

Now prepare and give a presentation to your partner as practice before you face the visitors. Remember that you should use the Passive when giving a presentation about a manufacturing process.

Start your presentation like this:

The milk is collected from local cows, and it is inspected and weighed.

8 Grammar test

1 Complete the sentences with *will, may, might, will not*, or *might not*. Each word or phrase can be used more than once. Use the words in brackets to help you.
   1 Cars of the future _____ be safer than today's cars. (certain)
   2 Future space travel _____ discover planets outside our solar system. (possible)
   3 Solar power _____ provide *some* of our energy needs. (certain)
   4 But solar power _____ meet *all* our needs because the sun doesn't shine everywhere all the time. (certain)
   5 Modern cars have two braking systems because a single braking system _____ work in an emergency. (possible)
   6 A lot of land vehicles _____ have hydrogen or hybrid engines by 2050. (possible)

2 Write questions for the answers, using the words in brackets. Do not repeat the words in *italics*.

   EXAMPLE   Staff will finish work tomorrow *at 2 p.m.* (When)
              When will staff finish work tomorrow?

   1 The office computers won't work today *because of a virus*. (Why)
   2 The boss will announce *a pay rise* next week. (What)
   3 The heating system will operate *using solar power*. (How)
   4 Wind farms might not provide enough power for us *because the wind isn't strong here*. (Why)
   5 *Air travel* will become more expensive as fuel costs increase. (What)
   6 Planes won't need so much fuel *because they will use more composites and so be lighter*. (Why)

3 Complete the dialogue with *may, might, will*, or *won't*. Each word can be used more than once.

   A I think the world's temperature _____ ¹ definitely rise by 10 °C by the year 2050.
   B I disagree. The temperature _____ ² rise by 10 °C – that's impossible. But it _____ ³ rise by 2 °C or possibly 3 °C – that's possible.
   A Well, maybe you're right. But one thing is certain. Oil _____ ⁴ run out in the next 30 years because there's very little oil left.
   B That's not certain at all. There's plenty of oil left. We _____ ⁵ have to dig deeper wells for the oil – that's possible. But I'm certain that oil _____ ⁶ run out in that time.
   A I just don't agree. I think we _____ ⁷ have to find alternative solutions. What do you think about solar power? One day we _____ ⁸ drive solar-powered cars.
   B That _____ ⁹ be the answer, especially in Britain; there aren't enough days of sunshine. I know it's dangerous but there's a possibility that nuclear power _____ ¹⁰ help.

8 Communication

1. Discuss the advantages and disadvantages of different types of fuel.
2. Complete the following table with your group.

	Advantages	Disadvantages
Petrol		
LPG		
Hydrogen		

Key to symbols on tables:

Scale: ✓✓ = Excellent ✓ = Good 0 = Fair ✗ = Bad

(Notes: *Efficiency* = low fuel consumption; *Range* = distance travelled after refuelling)

3. After you have completed the charts, have a conversation about the implications of using these fuels in the future. You have some extra notes to help you with the discussion.

✂--

Student A

		Carbons	Smoke	Power	Efficiency	Range
Normal fuel	Petrol	0	✓	✓	✓	✓

Notes: Experts believe that there is not much oil left in the world. There is more gas in the world than oil but it is not renewable. The only emission from hydrogen is water but it takes a lot of energy to produce hydrogen.

✂--

Student B

		Carbons	Smoke	Power	Efficiency	Range
Normal fuel	LPG	✓	✓	0	✓	✓

Notes: Experts believe that there is not much oil left in the world. There is more gas in the world than oil but it is not renewable. The only emission from hydrogen is water but it takes a lot of energy to produce hydrogen.

✂--

Student C

		Carbons	Smoke	Power	Efficiency	Range
Alternative fuel	Hydrogen	✓✓	✓✓	0	✓	✗

Notes: Experts believe that there is not much oil left in the world. There is more gas in the world than oil but it is not renewable. The only emission from hydrogen is water but it takes a lot of energy to produce hydrogen.

9 Grammar test

1 Make the warnings more formal. Use *must be* + Past Participle *(e.g. done)*.
(Note: only include the agent with *by* if you think the information is important.)

EXAMPLE   You have to wear this white coat in every part of the food processing factory.
This white coat must be worn in every part of the food processing factory.

1 You need to use these ear protectors everywhere in the aircraft hangar.
2 Specialist technicians should repair the computers.
3 Expert technicians should check this engine.
4 You must leave the wet concrete for several days before walking on it.
5 You need to lubricate these gears every day.

2 Rewrite the instructions using the words in brackets.

EXAMPLE   Always knock on the door before you come in.
You _____ (must)
You must knock on the door before you come in.

1 Drivers must check the brakes, lights, tyres, and water before a long car journey.
   _____ (required)
2 Apprentices are required to wear overalls in the workshop.
   Apprentices _____ (must / always)
3 Report all accidents to your supervisor.
   All accidents _____ (must)
4 Never work at a height without a harness and a lifeline.
   You _____ (must / not)
5 Always wear a safety helmet in this building site.
   A safety helmet _____ (must)

3 Rewrite the instructions using the words in brackets.

EXAMPLE   First check the guard is on the machine. Then switch it on. (always)
_____ before switching it on.
Always check the guard is on the machine before switching it on.

1 If you haven't closed down your program first, don't switch off your computer. (never)
   _____ without closing down your program first.
2 Only enter this warehouse after you've put on this overall and safety helmet. (don't)
   _____ without putting on this overall and safety helmet.
3 You must not eat or drink at the same time as you operate this machinery. (never)
   _____ while operating this machinery.
4 First fasten your safety belt. Then you can start the car and drive away. (only)
   _____ after fastening your safety belt.
5 Switch off the power to the video machine. Then you can take off the cover. (always)
   _____ before taking off the cover.

9 Communication

Accident survey form

Name of site: *Three Valleys Construction* Year: ....

A	Total number of accidents during year	....
B	Number of injuries from accident	....
C	Number of deaths from accident	....
D	Total number of observed breaches of safety rule	....
E	Enter number of breaches of each safety rule below	
1	No smoking is permitted anywhere on site.	....
2	Hard hats must be worn at all times.	....
3	Safety boots must always be worn on site.	....
4	Safety nets must be placed beneath floors with no deck.	....
5	Safety harnesses must be worn at heights.	....
6	Crane operators must always have an assistant.	....
7	Cables must be attached to crane loads.	....
8	Crane operator must check that the ground is level.	....

(Note: a breach of a safety rule means *breaking* a safety rule)

Student A
You are a Safety Inspector. You are carrying out a survey on safety procedures at a construction site. Interview the Site Manager and complete this survey form.

3 FINDINGS
These are our main findings about general safety at the *Three Valleys Construction* site.

1 We saw six workers walking around the site without safety helmets. We note that two accidents happened during the year, in which two workers without helmets had serious head injuries.

2 Safety shoes were also a problem. One worker wearing normal shoes had a serious injury to his feet when a concrete block fell on him.

3 There were two fires during the year, both caused by smokers throwing cigarettes into packing materials. One supervisor was seriously burnt.

4 One builder last year fell from a first floor and broke his leg. He had failed to fasten a safety harness and lifeline before starting work.

5 During inspections we saw three builders working on a high storey without a safety net below them.

6 Two months ago a crane turned over on its side because the ground was not level. The operator was slightly injured.

7 In another accident, the crane operator had no assistant helping him. The crane load swung out of control and struck another worker causing a serious injury to his arm.

8 In another incident with a crane, there was no cable attached to the load, and the crane load swung towards two workers. Fortunately they were not injured.

4 CONCLUSIONS

Student B
You are the Site Manager of a construction site. Read this extract from a report and answer the Safety Inspector's questions.

10 Grammar test

1 Join each pair of sentences using *which* or *who*.

EXAMPLE A solar panel is a device. This device converts sunlight into electrical power.
A solar panel is a device which converts sunlight into electrical power.

1 A nurse is an employee. This employee looks after patients.
2 Aspirin is a medicine. This medicine relieves pain.
3 A set of step-up gears is a mechanism. This mechanism increases the rate of rotation.
4 Paediatricians are doctors. These doctors treat children.
5 An operating table is a piece of hospital equipment. It supports patients during surgery.

2 Match the parts of the table.

item		function	
a artificial heart	machine	1	help blind people to move around easily
b X-ray technician	specialist	2	calculate the best heart rate for a patient
c the AbioCor controller	device	3	combine three types of engineering
d RP6	robot	4	operate and process X-rays
e ultracane	device	5	examine patients remotely
f mechatronics	field	6	pump blood around the body

3 Write sentences using information from the table.

EXAMPLE *An artificial heart is a machine which pumps blood around the body.*

4 Rewrite the sentences as dialogues.

EXAMPLE A can-opener is a device which opens metal cans.
A *What's this device for?* **B** *It's for opening metal cans.*

1 Sensors are components which detect changes in the environment.
2 An injection moulder is a machine which makes molten plastic into products.
3 Artificial hearts are devices which pump blood around the body and into the lungs.
4 A scanner is a machine which converts a visual image into digital form.
5 A hearing aid is a mechanism which increases the volume of sound waves in the ear.

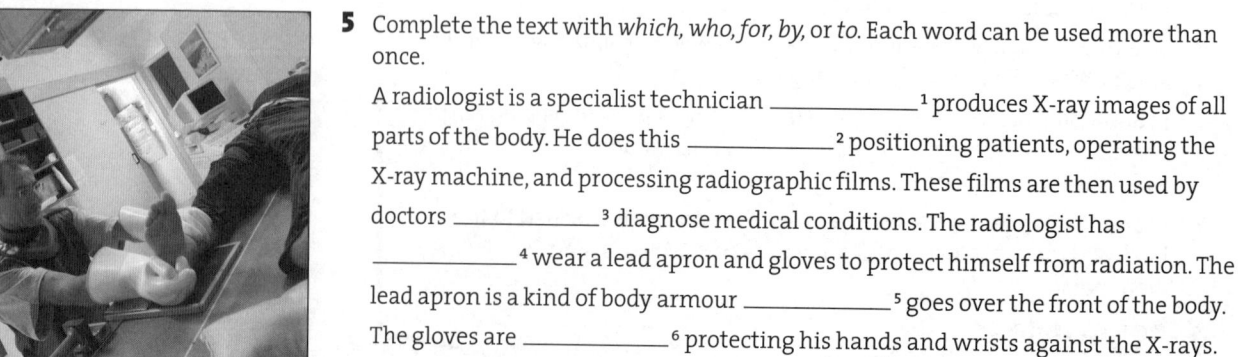

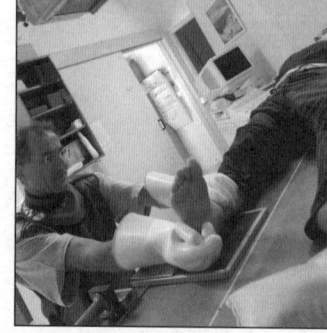

5 Complete the text with *which, who, for, by,* or *to*. Each word can be used more than once.

A radiologist is a specialist technician _____¹ produces X-ray images of all parts of the body. He does this _____² positioning patients, operating the X-ray machine, and processing radiographic films. These films are then used by doctors _____³ diagnose medical conditions. The radiologist has _____⁴ wear a lead apron and gloves to protect himself from radiation. The lead apron is a kind of body armour _____⁵ goes over the front of the body. The gloves are _____⁶ protecting his hands and wrists against the X-rays.

10 Communication

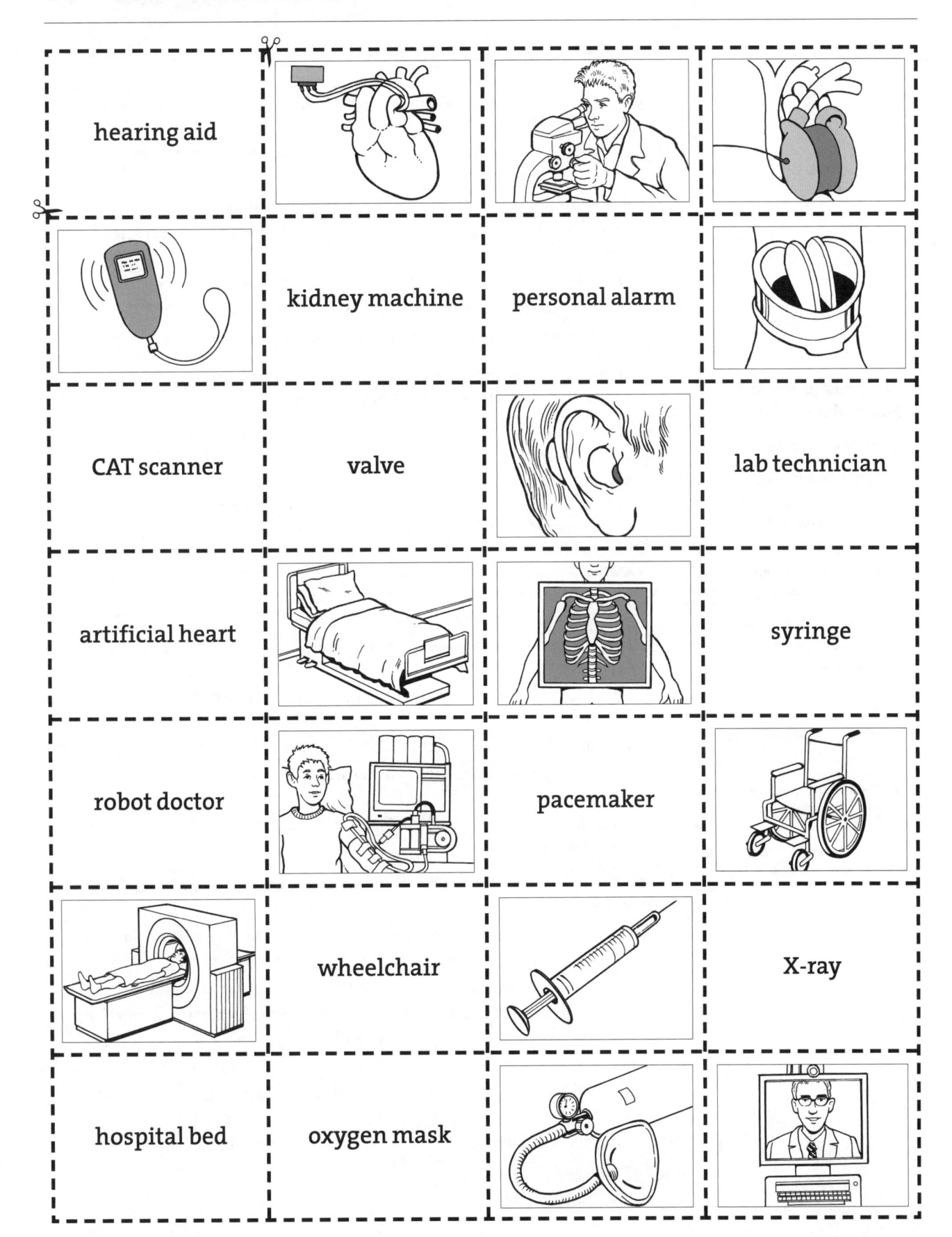

hearing aid			
	kidney machine	personal alarm	
CAT scanner	valve		lab technician
artificial heart			syringe
robot doctor		pacemaker	
	wheelchair		X-ray
hospital bed	oxygen mask		

11 Grammar test

1 Rewrite the advice as your personal opinion using *I think* or *I don't think* with *should*.

EXAMPLE You are advised not to look at a computer screen for more than 30 minutes.
I don't think you should look at a computer screen for more than 30 minutes.

1 It is advisable for you to shut down your computer and restart it.
2 I'd recommend that you don't touch that door for at least five hours after painting it.
3 Try using a socket wrench to take those wheel nuts off.
4 It's not a good idea for you to change your office computer system.
5 I suggest you don't use this machine until you've read the safety manual.

2 Read the extract from an instruction manual, then write some advice for a customer. Use each of these words and phrases once only.

You can …   Try …-ing   You should …
I suggest you …   Why don't you …?   I think you should …

EXAMPLE Shut down and restart your computer.
Why don't you shut down and restart your computer?

Customer problem # 4: Mouse does not work

Suggested solutions:

1 Check that the mouse is connected to the computer using the correct socket.
2 Reinstall the mouse driver using the CD.
3 Make sure that the mouse is compatible with the computer operating system (e.g. Windows XP).
4 Open Control Panel and check the mouse settings.
5 Install the mouse driver from the DOS prompt.

3 Write the questions for these answers. Begin: *Do you think we should …?*

EXAMPLE Yes, I think we should hire a guard. That would help the security problem in the factory.
Do you think we should hire a guard?

1 No, I don't think we should change our computer system. It would be too expensive.
2 I don't see why we shouldn't open a new company branch. It might increase our turnover.
3 Yes, I think the grinding machine should be repaired. It breaks down frequently.
4 Yes, the report should be written immediately. We can't start work until the report is ready.
5 No, I don't see why we should replace the injection moulder. It works well and never breaks down.

4 Give advice or instructions using *should*, *shouldn't*, *must*, or *mustn't*. Use the words in brackets to help you.

EXAMPLE Never use a naked light such as a match near to petrol or gas. (instruction)
You mustn't use a naked light such as a match near to petrol or gas.

1 Place the top of the monitor at eye level when working at a computer. (advice)
2 Always wear a hat and hair net when working in a food factory. (instruction)
3 Use a chair with good support for the back and neck when sitting at a desk. (advice)
4 Don't forget to wash your hands thoroughly after handling any chemicals. (instruction)
5 Don't play computer games for more than an hour per day. (advice)

11 Communication

Student A

1 You are a Computer Hotline Technician. Read the extract from your troubleshooting guide. A customer phones you with problems. Give the customer advice and instructions.

2 You are trying to set up a wireless network to link your notebook computer to a wireless router but you are having problems. Phone the computer hotline technician and note down the solutions he / she suggests. For example:

My notebook computer can't connect to the Internet wirelessly. What should I do?

My notebook connects to the Internet, but the signal strength is very low. What's the solution?

Problem:
The installation CD does not start automatically.

Solutions:
Recommended close other Windows programs first.
Essential click START and then click RUN. Type in D:\install.exe.

Problem:
The installation software cannot locate the wireless router.

Solutions:
Recommended close down any firewall and anti-virus program first.
Essential switch off power to the router for ten seconds, and then switch on again. Check the power light is on.
Recommended shut down and restart computer.
Essential re-start installation CD.

Student B

1 You are trying to set up a wireless network to link your notebook computer to a wireless router but you are having problems. Phone the computer hotline technician and note down the solutions he / she suggests. For example:

When I put the installation CD into the drive, the CD doesn't start automatically. What can I do?

The installation software is running, but it can't find the wireless router. What should I do?

2 You are a Computer Hotline Technician. Read the extract from your troubleshooting guide. A customer phones you with problems. Give the customer advice and instructions.

Problem:
The notebook computer is unable to connect wirelessly to the Internet.

Solutions:
Recommended close down wireless program and reopen. Check if there is a connection. If there is, move the notebook to a location where the connection is made.
Essential move notebook nearer router.

Problem 2:
The notebook computer connects to the Internet, but the signal strength is very low.

Solutions:
Recommended use notebook max. 30m from router.
Essential use notebook max. 60m from router.
Recommended move metal cabinets out of the way.
Essential move wireless telephone handsets away from router.

12 Grammar test

1 Write sentences using the Past Passive form of the verbs in brackets.

EXAMPLE   1971 First email (send)
The first email was sent in 1971.

1 1973 First mobile phone (produce)
2 1981 First space shuttle (launch)
3 1985 First version of Microsoft Windows (ship)
4 1990 First working version of World Wide Web (complete)
5 1996 First clockwork radio (invent)

2 Change the sentences from active to passive.

EXAMPLE   Before pens, people wrote letters using feathers dipped in ink.
Before pens, letters were written using feathers dipped in ink.

1 They completed the Akashi Kaikyo bridge in Japan in 1998.
2 People began work on the International Space Station (ISS) in 1998.
3 Space shuttles brought the first crew members to the ISS in 1999.
4 They flew the first supersonic aeroplane, Concorde, in 1969.

3 Match items from the past with contrasting items from the present.

Past	Present
a Paint cars by hand	1 graphite or titanium
b Carry phone messages by metal wires	2 inkjet or laser printers
c Make tennis rackets from wood	3 email and the Internet
d Print documents using dot matrix printers	4 computer-controlled spray
e Play music by means of tape recorders	5 fibre-optic cables
f Send letters using postal service	6 minidisks, CDs, and iPods

4 Write sentences using information from the table. Begin: *In the past ...*

EXAMPLE   *In the past, cars were painted by hand, but now they are painted using computer-controlled sprays.*

5 Ask relevant questions using the question words in brackets. Do not repeat the words in *italics*.

EXAMPLE   The suspension bridge was built *to link together two islands*. (Why)
Why was the suspension bridge built?

1 The first telephones were installed *in the 1880s*. (When)
2 Radar was first used *on ships sailing through icebergs*. (Where)
3 The first radios were powered *by means of large batteries*. (How)
4 Television was invented *in the early 20th century*. (When)
5 The space station was launched *to allow scientists to do experiments in space*. (Why)

12 Communication

1 Read the guide to codes and discuss it with your group until you are sure you understand how the two codes work.

Here are two different ways to code the same message.
Real message: CARS ARE DESIGNED BY COMPUTER
Coded message using method 1: EDE BYC UTE SAR OMP NED CAR RXY SIG
Coded message using method 2: XVMNV MZYZN DBIZY WTXJH KPOZM

How do they work?

Method 1   Real message: CARS ARE DESIGNED BY COMPUTER

CAR	SAR	EDE	SIG	NED	BYC	OMP	UTE	RXY
1	2	3	4	5	6	7	8	9
3	6	8	2	7	5	1	9	4
EDE	BYC	UTE	SAR	OMP	NED	CAR	RXY	SIG

Key: 123456789 (real message) ➲ 368275194 (coded message)

Procedure:
1 Divide the message into groups of three letters.
2 Add 'dummy' letters (e.g. X, Y, or Z) at the end to complete a group.
3 Change the order of the groups, using the key.

Method 2   Real message: CARS ARE DESIGNED BY COMPUTER

CARSA	REDES	IGNED	BYCOM	PUTER
XVMNV	MZYZN	DBIZY	WTXJH	KPOZM

Key: Move the alphabet forward by five characters:
    A B C D E F G H I J K L M N O P Q R S T U V W X Y Z (real message)
➲ V W X Y Z A B C D E F G H I J K L M N O P Q R S T U (coded message)

Procedure:
1 Divide the message into groups of five letters.
2 If necessary, add 'dummy' letters (e.g. X, Y, Z) at the end to complete a group (not needed here).
3 Change each letter to another letter, using the key.

2 With your group, solve these coded messages. Each message uses one of the two methods shown above, but with a different key. The messages are all taken from the reading passage on p.87 of the Student's Book. They are the names of items of equipment or processes used in the design and manufacture of cars.

1 IDE ERA PUT DDE NXZ SIG COM
2 DMA URI ERA NGZ ACT PUT COM IDE NUF
3 FRPSX WHUQX PHULF DOFRQ WUROO HGZAX
4 EQORW VGTKP VGITC VGFOC PWHCE VWTKP IZAZB

3 With your group, devise a new code system. Write your system out clearly like the ones in 1. Make sure you write out the procedure and the key.

4 Write a short sentence (approximately 20–25 letters) in your new code. Remember to add 'dummy' letters if the last group of letters is too short. Give your coded message to one of the other groups, and time how long they take to 'crack' the code. Take the sentence from one of the exercises in the Student's Book.

13 Grammar test

1 Complete the sentences about a brother and a sister, Roberto and Renata, using the Present Perfect or Past Simple form of the verbs in brackets.

1. Roberto _____ (be) a computer technician for the last three years.
2. During this time, he _____ (set up) five networks for large companies.
3. Before becoming a computer technician, he _____ (be) a computer repair man in a shop for four years.
4. During those four years he _____ (repair) hundreds of computers.
5. Since 2006 he _____ (work) for Dynatron, the biggest company in the region.
6. Roberto and Renata both _____ (become) interested in computers while they were at school.
7. In September 2006, Renata _____ (begin) a university course in computer science.
8. Over the last three months Renata _____ (take) three exams.

2 Look at the table. Complete the answers with *since* or *for*, then write the questions. Begin: *How long …?*

EXAMPLE
A *How long has the International Space Station (ISS) been in space?*
B *It has been in space **since** 1998.*
A *How long did the manned missions to the Moon continue?*
B *They continued **for** three years.*

1. They have travelled to space stations _____ 1981.
2. It remained in space _____ fifteen years.
3. They have flown to Mars _____ 1960.
4. They have orbited Earth _____ 1957.
5. It has been in space _____ 1990.
6. The mission was in space _____ fourteen years.

Project	Started	Finished?
International Space Station in space	1998	No
Manned missions to the Moon	1969	Yes, 1972
1 Space shuttles to space stations	1981	No
2 Russian Mir space station in space	1986	Yes, 2001
3 Space missions to Mars	1965	No
4 Satellites orbiting Earth	1957	No
5 Hubble Space Telescope	1990	No
6 Galileo Mission to planet Jupiter	1989	Yes, 2003

13 Communication

Group A

Frequently Asked Questions about VoIP

What are the main advantages of VoIP?

- VoIP is much cheaper than telephone. VoIP has a small flat-rate charge for all calls, including long-distance and international.
- You can talk with many people in different places at the same time. Online meetings are easy.
- Pictures, videos, music files can be sent at the same time.
- Online customer support is quicker and better than with telephone landlines or mobile phones.

- VoIP is portable – you can call from anywhere in the world by logging into your account on the computer. Your phone number is the same everywhere.
- The hardware is small and lightweight – headset or small IP phone.
- VoIP has excellent coverage all over the world. Compare this with poor coverage of mobile phones in some parts of the world.

Add any other advantages you have discovered in your own research.
_____
_____

What arguments do you think Group B will make? Note the points you could make against these arguments.
_____
_____

Group B

Frequently Asked Questions about VoIP

What are the main disadvantages of VoIP?

- VoIP only works if your computer is switched on and the software is running. The other person must have the same software loaded and running on his / her computer.
- Some VoIP companies only allow you to call someone subscribing to the same company.
- The sound quality can be poor – delay, echo, silent patches.
- If a company changes to VoIP, it has to buy headsets or internet phones – expensive.

- If there is a power cut, you can't use VoIP (unless you have battery back-up). Landline phone stays on because of current in phone line.
- Difficult to use for emergency services – the operator cannot locate your address.
- You must have a second computer set up if you want to run a second phone line.
- VoIP can only be used with broadband connection.

Add any other disadvantages you have discovered in your own research.
_____
_____

What arguments do you think Group A will make? Note the points you could make against these arguments.
_____
_____

14 Grammar test

1 Rewrite the statements using *must*, *mustn't*, *should*, or *shouldn't*.

EXAMPLE   A requirement for all applicants for this job is a degree in Engineering.
All applicants for this job must have a degree in Engineering.

1 It is essential that candidates for the job are not over 65 years old.
2 Preference will be given to applicants who do not smoke.
3 Applicants for this post are required to be good team players.
4 Speaking a foreign language by candidates is preferable.
5 It is essential that applicants do not live more than ten miles from London.

2 Put a tick in the correct box next to each question.

	What the questioner expects ...		
	Information	Yes or No	Longer answer
1 What's your full name?	✓		
2 Do you hold a driving licence?			
3 When did you get your diploma?			
4 Where did you study for your diploma?			
5 Did you enjoy the course?			
6 What was your favourite subject?			
7 What did you like about it?			
8 Why do you want this job?			

3 Complete these questions an interviewer asked Aisha Chetty (see Student's Book p.101). Use the verbs in brackets.

1 Where _____ (work) now?
2 How long _____ (work) at Western IT?
3 Have _____ (work) for any other companies?
4 When _____ (gain) your HND?
5 Where _____ (go) to college?
6 What subjects _____ (study) at college?
7 How long _____ (study) for your HND?
8 Why _____ (organize) a class visit to France Telecom?

14 Communication

1. With your whole group, complete this job advertisement giving details of a job which the interviewee would like to apply for.

2. Now divide your group into two sub-groups: A is the interviewing panel, B is the interviewee.

_____¹ is looking for a _____² to join a team of _____³ based in the city of _____⁴. Candidates preferably should have a Certificate or Diploma in _____⁵, but other technical areas will be considered. Additional practical skills in _____⁶ would be an advantage. Candidates must be prepared to work irregular hours and to travel. Experience working in _____⁷ is an advantage but not essential. The successful candidate will be able to work well in a team, and have good communication skills.

---

¹Name of company:
 (e.g. *Network Solutions Co Ltd*)

²Job title:
 (e.g. *Software Technician*)

³Other job titles in team:
 (e.g. *IT Specialists*)

⁴Name of city:

⁵Field of study:
 (e.g. *Software Engineering*)

⁶Practical skills:
 (e.g. *electrical installation*)

⁷Work experience:
 (e.g. *computer or electronics companies*)

✂- -

Group A: Interviewing panel

Prepare questions to ask the interviewee in the job interview. Also make notes on what your company gives its employees.

Notes	Questions
subjects studied? favourite subjects? reasons? work experience? enjoy work experience? skills learned?	Which subjects did you study in your diploma? Which subjects did you enjoy most in your course? Why did you enjoy that subject most?
training salary benefits (e.g. healthcare)	

✂- -

Group B: Interviewee

Prepare a list of points you want to make, and some questions to ask the interviewing panel, in the job interview.

Notes	Statements
favourite subjects strengths work experience what I learned	My favourite subject was _____. I enjoyed this subject because _____. My main strength is _____.

Notes	Questions
training? salary? benefits (e.g. healthcare)?	Do you give any training for the job?

15 Grammar test

1 Complete the table, changing the noun phrase in *italics* to a pronoun (*it* or *them*).

Phrasal verb	used with a *noun object*	used with a *pronoun object*
plug in	Have you plugged in *the adapter*?	Have you plugged *it* in?
print out	Please print out *these documents* for me.	Please print *them* out for me.
1 switch off	Did you switch off *the machines*?	Did you _____ ?
2 set up	Let's set up *the company* quickly.	Let's _____ quickly.
3 close down	Close down *the computers* immediately.	Close _____ immediately.
4 carry out	I'll carry out *the survey* tomorrow.	I'll _____ tomorrow.

2 Match phrasal verbs with their opposites. Complete the phrasal verbs with *on, out, off, together, up,* or *down*.

a push in the button
b switch the power on
c take off your goggles
d put your tools down
e open up the shop
f take the engine apart

1 put the machine _____ again
2 pick the hammer _____
3 pull *out* the plug
4 close _____ the office
5 turn _____ the lights
6 put _____ your helmet

3 Replace the verb in *italics* with the correct form of *set up, give up, plug in, find out, carry out, work out, put on,* or *take off*.

EXAMPLE   We hope to *implement* the new plan in the next financial year.
          We hope to carry out the new plan in the next financial year.

1 The safety inspectors hope to *discover* what caused the accident.
2 The video machine isn't working because you haven't *connected* to the power.
3 We need to *create* a new project team to design the new product.
4 The investigators have *stopped* their search for the missing documents.
5 One of a technician's jobs is to *calculate* the costs of a project or new product.

4 Write informal questions. Replace the verbs in *italics* with the active form of *cut down, work out, set up, find out,* or *put together*.

EXAMPLE   The speed of the crash *was calculated* using sensors and cameras.
          How did you work out the speed of the crash?

1 Many interesting facts *were discovered* during the investigation.
2 The computer parts *are assembled* in Workshop D.
3 The pollution from these chimneys *was reduced* by attaching filters to them.
4 This organization *was started* to develop young businesswomen as entrepreneurs.

15 Communication

Your group is a team of inventors taking part in a competition to find the best new technology for the future. With your team, prepare and give a short presentation about your idea for the future. Try to persuade a funding committee that your idea is the best.

Technology of the Future Competition: Team 1

New technology	Carbon fibre + nanotechnology
Industry	Bridge building
Possible date of use	2040?
How it will be used	Microscopic tubes made of pure carbon, a thousand times thinner than a human hair, twisted into cables
Advantages	Cables 100 times stronger than steel, one-sixtieth the weight
Main application	Ultra-long bridges, up to 200 km long
Other applications	Super-skyscrapers over a km high
Today's technology	Steel
Limits to today's technology	Not strong enough for very long bridges (> 5 km)

Your group is a team of inventors taking part in a competition to find the best new technology for the future. With your team, prepare and give a short presentation about your idea for the future. Try to persuade a funding committee that your idea is the best.

Technology of the Future Competition: Team 2

New technology	Active contact lenses
Industry	Virtual reality
Possible date of use	2020?
How it will be used	Tiny lasers on contact lenses scan 3-D image onto retina of eye
Advantages	No bulky equipment (headset, computer) needed
Main application	Instant information while travelling, shopping, etc.
Other applications	Realistic computer games merging with real world
Today's technology	Computer software, large headset, sensors, controls
Limits to today's technology	Heavy headset causes headache and eye strain

---

Your group is a team of inventors taking part in a competition to find the best new technology for the future. With your team, prepare and give a short presentation about your idea for the future. Try to persuade a funding committee that your idea is the best.

Technology of the Future Competition: Team 3

New technology	Giant mirrors floating in space
Industry	Artificial lighting
Possible date of use	2035?
How it will be used	Mirrors (60m diameter) reflect sunlight to Earth
Advantages	Free natural resource, more powerful than electricity
Main application	Increase growing time in agriculture
Other applications	Lighting for emergency staff in natural disasters
Today's technology	Electricity from oil, gas, nuclear power stations
Limits to today's technology	Not strong enough, expensive, drains natural resources

Grammar tests key

Unit 1

1
1. cheap / fast
2. cheaper / faster
3. large / safe
4. larger / safer
5. big / slim
6. bigger / slimmer
7. early / noisy
8. earlier / noisier
9. bad / far
10. worse / farther (or further)
11. combustible / portable
12. more combustible / more portable

2
1. … older than the saloon car.
2. … faster than the saloon car.
3. … more slowly than the sports car.
4. … smaller … than the saloon car.
5. … more expensive than the sports car.

3
1. mechanism, mechanic
2. technician, technology
3. electrical, electricity
4. engineering, engineer
5. electronics, electronic

Unit 2

1
2 C – PS	6 B – PC	10 B – PC
3 B – PC	7 D – PS	11 C – PS
4 D – PS	8 C – PS	12 D – PS
5 A – PS	9 A – PS	

2 The verbs that change are:
is controlling ➔ controls   is warming ➔ warms
are carrying ➔ carry   is flowing ➔ flows

3
1. am
2. study
3. attend
4. carry out
5. are doing
6. am working
7. installs
8. am helping
9. are visiting
10. is building

Unit 3

1
1. What / How much do the headphones weigh?
2. Does the weight include the cables?
3. Is the headband adjustable?
4. How wide is the ear cushion?
5. Does it (the box) include an extension cord?
6. How long is the cord?
7. Do the headphones use batteries or electricity?
8. How many batteries do they use?
9. How do you carry the headphones?
10. What is the total price?

2 Possible answers
2. Why did he design it?
3. When was the CD player designed?
4. How wide is it?
5. How thick is it?
6. What colour is it?
7. Which company sells it?
8. Can I buy it online?
9. How much does the shipping cost?
10. What is the total price?

Unit 4

1 1 to   2 of   3 for   4 to, to   5 from   6 for

2
1. Composites are made from plastic and many fibres.
2. Fibreglass is used for making the hulls of sailing boats.
3. The sails of sailing boats are made of polyester.
4. Bicycle helmets are made from polycarbonate and polystyrene.

3
1. is
2. returns
3. to
4. is
5. resistant
6. resists
7. has
8. is
9. flexible
10. bends

Grammar tests key

4
1. Fibreglass is tough and slightly flexible. This is why it is used to make arrows.
2. Polystyrene has good heat-resistance and lightness. This is why it is used for manufacturing the insides of bike helmets.
3. Polycarbonate is transparent and highly scratch-resistant. This is why it is used to make sunglasses.
4. Titanium is hard and is corrosion-resistant. This is why it is used to make ship propellers.

Unit 5

1 and **2**

- a – 7 When you press the alarm button, a loud bell rings.
- b – 8 As you turn the steering wheel clockwise, the car turns to the right.
- c – 5 When you click on the 'save' button, the program stores your data on the hard disk.
- d – 4 As you turn the steering wheel anti-clockwise, the car moves to the left.
- e – 6 As the pendulum of the clock oscillates, the spring becomes tighter.
- f – 1 When you push down the camera button, the camera takes a picture.
- g – 3 As the piston moves in a reciprocating motion, it turns the camshaft in a rotary movement.
- h – 2 As you rotate the volume knob clockwise, the sound on the radio becomes louder.

3
1. before 3. after 5. before
2. after 4. after 6. after

4
1. As the piston moves down the cylinder, the oil in the pipe transmits pressure to the brake pad.
2. When the pressure of the oil pushes the pad against the disc, the wheel slows down and stops.
3. When you release the brake pedal, the piston moves up the cylinder towards the pedal.
4. As the piston returns up the cylinder, it removes pressure from the oil in the pipe.
5. When the pads move away from the disc, the wheel is able to move freely.

Unit 6

1
1. The GPS navigation system locates your position anywhere on earth.
2. The Rotundus spherical robot patrols and guards buildings and sites.
3. The Flashcam warns people not to commit a crime.
4. Dynamic grip recognition allows a gun to be used only by its owner.
5. A police officer protects the public and catches criminals.

2
1. protecting   4. to incapacitate
2. detect   5. monitoring
3. protection   6. warn

3 1 for 2 to 3 for 4 as 5 to 6 as 7 to 8 as

Unit 7

1 Possible answer

First, the plug is pushed into the socket. Then, the scart cable is connected between the TV and DVD player. Then, two AAA batteries are inserted into the remote control. Next, the power is switched on. Then, the TV channel is set to AV. Now, the OPEN/CLOSE button on the DVD player is pressed to open the door. Next, a disc is placed onto the door. Finally, the OPEN/CLOSE button is touched again to close the door.

2
1. Steel plates are bonded using different types of welding (by welders).
2. Loaves are removed from their tins by suction devices.
3. Plastic parts are moulded using extrusion or other processes.
4. Loaves are sliced in a high-speed slicing machine by huge saw blades.
5. The hopper is filled first.
6. Plastic parts are removed from the mould when they are cold.

3
1. The plastic is melted using heaters.
2. The melted plastic is pushed along the barrel using a ram.
3. Dough is made to rise using yeast.
4. The loaves are taken out of their tins using suction.
5. The loaves are sliced using giant saw blades.

4 1 by 2 from 3 to 4 in 5 to 6 by

Unit 8

1
1. will
2. may / might
3. will
4. will not
5. may / might not
6. may / might

2
1. Why won't the office computers work today?
2. What will the boss announce next week?
3. How will the heating system operate?
4. Why might wind farms not provide enough power for us?
5. What will become more expensive as fuel costs increase?
6. Why won't planes need so much fuel?

3
1. will
2. won't
3. may / might
4. will
5. may / might
6. won't
7. will
8. may / might
9. won't
10. may / might

Unit 9

1
1. These ear protectors must be used everywhere in the aircraft hangar.
2. The computers must be repaired by specialist technicians.
3. This engine must be checked by expert technicians.
4. The wet concrete must be left for several days before walking on it.
5. These gears must be lubricated every day.

2
1. Drivers are required to check the brakes, lights, tyres, and water before a long car journey.
2. Apprentices must always wear overalls in the workshop.
3. All accidents must be reported to your supervisor.
4. You must not work at a height without a harness and a lifeline.
5. A safety helmet must always be worn in this building site.

3
1. Never switch off your computer …
2. Don't enter this warehouse …
3. Never eat or drink …
4. Only start the car and drive away …
5. Always switch off the power to the video machine …

Unit 10

1
1. A nurse is an employee who looks after patients.
2. Aspirin is a medicine which relieves pain.
3. A set of step-up gears is a mechanism which increases the rate of rotation.
4. Paediatricians are doctors who treat children.
5. An operating table is a piece of hospital equipment which supports patients during surgery.

2 and **3**
- b – 4 An X-ray technician is a specialist who operates and processes X-rays.
- c – 2 The AbioCor controller is a device which calculates the best heart rate for a patient.
- d – 5 An RP6 is a robot which examines patients remotely.
- e – 1 Ultracane is a device which helps blind people to move around easily.
- f – 3 Mechatronics is a field which combines three types of engineering.

4
1. A What are these components for?
   B They're for detecting changes in the environment.
2. A What's this machine for?
   B It's for making molten plastic into products.
3. A What are these devices for?
   B They're for pumping blood around the body and into the lungs.
4. A What's this machine for?
   B It's for converting a visual image into digital form.
5. A What's this mechanism for?
   B It's for increasing the volume of sound waves in the ear.

5 1 who 2 by 3 to 4 to 5 which 6 for

Unit 11

1
1. I think you should close down your computer and restart it now.
2. I don't think you should touch that door for at least five hours after painting it.
3. I think you should use a socket wrench to take those wheel nuts off.
4. I don't think you should change your office computer system.
5. I don't think you should use this machine until you've read the safety manual.

2 Possible answers
1 I suggest you check that the mouse is connected to the computer using the correct socket.
2 You can reinstall the mouse driver using the CD.
3 I think you should make sure that the mouse is compatible with Windows XP.
4 Try opening Control Panel and checking the mouse settings.
5 You should install the mouse driver from the DOS prompt.

3 Do you think we should …
1 … change our computer system?
2 … open a new company branch?
3 … repair the grinding machine?
4 … write the report immediately?
5 … replace the injection moulder?

4
1 You should place the top of the monitor at eye level when working at a computer.
2 You must wear a hat and hair net when working in a food factory.
3 You should use a chair with good support for the back and neck when sitting at a desk.
4 You must wash your hands thoroughly after handling any chemicals.
5 You shouldn't play computer games for more than an hour per day.

Unit 12

1
1 The first mobile phone was produced in 1973.
2 The first space shuttle was launched in 1981.
3 The first version of Microsoft Windows was shipped in 1985.
4 The first working version of the World Wide Web was completed in 1990.
5 The first clockwork radio was invented in 1996.

2
1 The Akashi Kaikyo bridge in Japan was completed in 1998.
2 Work on the International Space Station was begun in 1998.
3 The first crew members were brought to the ISS in 1999 by space shuttles.
4 The first supersonic aeroplane, Concorde, was flown in 1969.

3 b–5 c–1 d–2 e–6 f–3

4
b In the past, phone messages were carried by metal wires, but now they are carried by fibre-optic cables.
c In the past, tennis rackets were made from wood, but now they are made from graphite or titanium.
d In the past, documents were printed using dot matrix printers, but now they are printed using inkjet or laser printers.
e In the past, music was played on tape recorders, but now it is played on minidisks, CDs, and iPods.
f In the past, letters were sent using the postal service, but now they are sent using email and the Internet.

5
1 When were the first telephones installed?
2 Where was radar first used?
3 How were the first radios powered?
4 When was television invented?
5 Why was the space station launched?

Unit 13

1
1 has been   5 has worked
2 has set up   6 became
3 was   7 began
4 repaired   8 has taken

2
1 A How long have space shuttles travelled to space stations?
  B They have travelled to space stations **since** 1981.
2 A How long did the Russian Mir space station remain in space?
  B It remained in space **for** fifteen years.
3 A How long have space missions flown to Mars?
  B They have flown to Mars **since** 1965.
4 A How long have satellites orbited Earth?
  B They have orbited Earth **since** 1957.
5 A How long has the Hubble Space Telescope been in space?
  B It has been in space **since** 1990.
6 A How long was the Galileo Mission in space?
  B The mission was in space **for** fourteen years.

Unit 14

1
1. Candidates for the job mustn't be over 65 years old.
2. Applicants shouldn't smoke.
3. Applicants for this post must be good team players.
4. Candidates should speak a foreign language.
5. Applicants mustn't live more than ten miles from London.

2
2. yes / no
3. info
4. info
5. yes / no
6. info
7. longer
8. longer

3
1. … do you work …
2. … have you worked …
3. … you worked …
4. … did you gain …
5. … did you go …
6. … did you study …
7. … did you study …
8. … did you organize …

Unit 15

1
1. Did you switch them off?
2. Let's set it up quickly.
3. Close them down immediately.
4. I'll carry it out tomorrow.

2
b – 5 – off
c – 6 – on
d – 2 – up
e – 4 – down
f – 1 – together

3
1. find out
2. plugged in
3. set up
4. given up
5. work out

4 Possible answers
1. What did you find out during the investigation?
2. Where do they put together the computer parts?
3. How did you cut down the pollution from these chimneys?
4. Why did you set up this organization?